Summer Homes Among The Mountains: On The New York, Ontario And Western Railway

J. E. Childs

In the interest of creating a more extensive selection of rare historical book reprints, we have chosen to reproduce this title even though it may possibly have occasional imperfections such as missing and blurred pages, missing text, poor pictures, markings, dark backgrounds and other reproduction issues beyond our control. Because this work is culturally important, we have made it available as a part of our commitment to protecting, preserving and promoting the world's literature. Thank you for your understanding.

Summer Homes
Among the Mountains

On the New York, Ontario & Western Railway

J. E. CHILDS,
General Manager,

J. C. ANDERSON,
General Passenger Agent,

56 BEAVER ST., N. Y.

US 15448.45.
US 15438.92

By exchange
(New York Public Library)

COPYRIGHTED BY
J. C. ANDERSON, GENERAL PASSENGER AGENT,
NEW YORK, ONT. & WEST'N R'Y,
1892.

THE PRINTING DONE BY
WYNKOOP & HALLENBECK,
441 TO 447 PEARL ST.,
NEW YORK.

THE COVER AND THE HALF-TONE
ILLUSTRATIONS IN THIS BOOK ENGRAVED BY THE
PHOTOCHROME ENGRAVING CO.,
219-222 FULTON ST.,
NEW YORK.

INDEX TO STATIONS AND POST-OFFICES.

	Page		Page		Page
Accord,	30	Hamden,	126	Parksville,	105
Apex,	123	Hamilton,	138	Phillipsport,	48
		Hancock,	116	Pine Bush,	35
Beaverkill,	110	Harvard,	115	Pleasant Mount,	120
Beerston,	125	Hasbrouck,	66	Poyntelle,	119
Belmont,	120	Highland,	31	Pratt's,	141
Bernhard's Bay,	144	High View,	41	Preston Park,	119
Binnewater,	30	Horton,	113		
Bloomingburgh,	37	Huguenot,	47	Randallsville,	138
Bridgeville,	67	Hurleyville,	75	Rockdale,	133
Briscoe,	98			Rock Hill,	46
Burlingham,	43	Jeffersonville,	98	Rockland,	110
Burnside,	21			Rock Rift,	123
Butternut Grove,	113	Kenwood,	141	Rock Tavern,	20
				Rome,	140
Campbell Hall,	21	Lake Como,	119	Roscoe,	112
Cannonsville,	123	Lake Minnewaska,	28	Rosendale,	30
Carbondale,	121	Lake Mohonk,	26	Rutsonville,	25
Carpenter's Eddy	123	Lakin,	119		
Central Square,	145	Lew Beach,	110	Scranton,	121
Centreville,	62	Liberty,	83	Sidney,	132
Cleveland,	144	Liberty Falls,	80	Sidney Centre,	132
Clinton,	139	Little Britain,	20	South Fallsburgh,	65
Clintondale,	31	Livingston Manor,	108	South New Berlin,	134
Colchester,	113	Loch Sheldrake,	78	Spring Glen,	48
Como,	119	Loomis,	125	Springtown,	26
Constantia,	144			Starlight,	119
Cook's Falls,	112	Maplewood,	66	Stevensville,	81
Crystal Run,	32	McDonough,	137	Stony Ford,	32
Cuddebackville,	47	Meadow Brook,	19	Summitville,	46
		Mechanicstown,	33	Sylvan Beach,	143
De Bruce,	110	Meredith,	129		
De Lancey,	126	Mexico,	147	Thompsonville,	67
Delhi,	127	Middletown,	34	Trout Creek,	132
Divine's Corners,	78	Modena,	25		
Downsville,	115	Mohonk Lake,	26	Ulster Heights,	63
		Mongaup Valley,	66	Uniondale,	120
Earlville,	137	Montgomery,	22	Utica,	139
East Branch,	113	Monticello,	70		
Eaton,	141	Morrisville,	141	Walden,	23
Edmeston,	134	Mountain Dale,	59	Walker Valley,	43
Ellenville,	50	Mt. Meenahga,	53	Wallkill,	24
		Mt. Upton,	133	Walnut Mountain,	83
Fallsburgh,	63			Walton,	123
Florence,	140	Napanoch,	58	Wawonda,	85
Forest City,	120	Neversink,	97	West Cornwall,	18
Franklin,	130	New Berlin,	134	West Eaton,	141
Fruit Valley,	147	New Paltz,	25	West Monroe,	145
Fulton,	145	North Bay,	144	White Lake,	102
		Norwich,	137	White Port,	30
Galeville Mills,	24			White Sulphur Springs,	100
Gardiner,	24	Oneida,	142	Winterton,	35
Genung's,	20	Oriskany Falls,	138	Woodbourne,	69
Gilbertsville,	134	Orr's Mills,	19	Wurtsboro,	45
Glen Wild,	63	Oswego,	146		
Grahamsville,	66	Oxford,	135	Youngsville,	98
Greenfield,	55				
Guilford,	135				

DEPOTS AND FERRIES

······) OF THE (······

New York, ONTARIO & Western

RAILWAY COMPANY

IN NEW YORK

······) ARE LOCATED AT (······

FOOT OF W. 42D ST. AND FOOT OF FRANKLIN ST., N. R.

Agents of the New York Transfer Co. will call for baggage, furnish tickets, and check baggage from residence to destination.

Time Tables, Tickets and Information obtained at the following offices:

IN NEW YORK CITY.

No. 47 Broadway.
No. 323 Broadway.
No. 944 Broadway, near Madison Square.
No. 737 Sixth Avenue, cor. 42d Street.
No. 1323 Broadway, near 34th Street.
No. 1170 Ninth Avenue.
No. 134 East 125th Street, Harlem.
No. 264 West 125th Street, Harlem.
N. Y., O. & W. R'y, Foot of West 42d Street.
N. Y., O. & W. R'y, Foot of Franklin Street.

IN BROOKLYN.

No. 4 Court Street.
No. 860 Fulton Street.
Brooklyn Annex Office, Foot of Fulton Street.
No. 98 Broadway, Williamsburgh.
No. 107 Broadway, Williamsburgh.
No. 253 Manhattan Avenue, Greenpoint.
No. 215 Atlantic Avenue.

IN HOBOKEN.

No. 254 Washington Street.

RETURN PORTION OF EXCURSION TICKETS FROM LIBERTY AND STATIONS SOUTH ARE GOOD ONE YEAR FROM DATE OF SALE; NORTH OF LIBERTY GOOD FOR 30 DAYS.

Special Rates for Summer Travel.

We have prepared, and placed on sale, the following forms of tickets for parties desiring to make frequent trips to the country during the summer months.

CONDITIONS, LIMITS, Etc.

The TWENTY-FOUR TRIP TICKETS are good for individuals and families; are on sale from June 1st to September 30th, and are good for return passage up to and including October 31st, 1892.

The SIX ROUND TRIP TICKETS are only issued to individuals, and time limits the same as twenty-four ride tickets.

The above tickets are only good for continuous passage, and are not transferable. They will be found on sale at the General Passenger Office, 56 Beaver Street, and General Eastern Office, 323 Broadway. They may also be ordered through any ticket agent of this Company.

	Rates for 6 Round Trips	Rates for 24 Trip Tickets		Rates for 6 Round Trips	Rates for 24 Trip Tickets
West Cornwall,	$8.70	.....	Mountain Dale	$19.85	$37.20
Orr's Mills,	8.70	.....	Centreville,	21.00	38.65
Meadow Brook,	9.00	$21.60	Fallsburgh,	21.85	39.60
Denniston's,	9.75	22.35	Hurleyville,	22.70	41.05
Genung's,	10.60	23.05	Liberty Falls,	24.45	42.95
Rock Tavern,	11.30	24.25	Liberty,	25.00	43.70
Burnside,	11.55	24.50	Parksville,	26.45	45.35
Campbell Hall,	12.30	24.65	Livingston Manor,	27.90	47.55
Stony Ford,	12.30	24.65	Rockland,	28.00	49.70
Crystal Run,	12.30	24.65	Cook's Falls,	29.40	51.85
Mechanicstown,	12.30	24.65	Trout Brook,	31.30	54.50
Middletown,	12.30	24.65	East Branch,	32.10	55.20
Winterton,	14.00	31.70	Fish's Eddy,	32.85	56.65
Bloomingburgh,	14.40	32.85	Hancock Junction,	34.50	58.80
Wurtsboro,	16.65	33.10	Apex,	36.40	61.20
Summitville,	17.55	34.55	Rock Rift,	36.45	62.65
Phillipsport,	18.10	35.05	Walton,	36.70	65.55
Spring Glen,	18.65	35.65	Hamden,	37.15	68.90
Ellenville,	19.85	37.20	Delhi,	37.80	71.75

J. C. ANDERSON,
General Passenger Agent.

O'ER HILL AND DALE

THE object in publishing this book is to bring those residents of our cities, who have not only the desire but the intention of finding a desirable summer home, into communication with those having such to offer. Dealing with much of the most charming scenery of the Hudson river, and the beautiful and populous uplands of New York traversed by the New York, Ontario & Western Railway, there is room for the most concise statement of fact only. The region traversed includes Rockland, Orange, Sullivan, part of Ulster, Delaware, Chenango, part of Otsego, Madison, western Oneida and Oswego counties— a section abounding in beauty, with its mountain summits rising three thousand feet above the sea; its narrow, exquisitely lovely valleys; its numberless streams and waterfalls, its gem-like lakes; its rugged hillsides, with their heavy growth of forest woods; its quiet nooks, and its abundant game to reward the sportsman's toil. The whole region is free from malarial fevers, which are now proving so formidable and pestilential in all our large cities. The greater part of it is above the level of hay-fever and rose-colds, and its comparative dryness and uniformity of temperature, and the resinous perfume of the pines, hemlocks and cedars, make it a desirable region, at least in the summer and early autumn, for persons afflicted with pulmonary or rheumatic diseases.

The New York *World*, on August 6th and 7th, 1890, secured a thermometer test of the principal mountain resorts with the following results:

		8.00 A.M.	12.00 M.	3.00 P.M.	8.00 P.M.
RICHFIELD SPRINGS	August 6th,	69°	75½°	76°	71°
" "	" 7th,	62°	68½°	72½°	70°
SARATOGA	" 6th,	75°	76°	80°	74°
"	" 7th,	68°	72°	76°	74°
MOUNT McGREGOR	" 6th,	65°	69°	68°	66°
" "	" 7th,	64°	67°	67°	65°
LIBERTY	" 6th,	64°	74°	74°	66°
"	" 7th,	6.°	72°	74°	63°

What Medical Experts Say.

THE following is copied from the Hand-Book of Historical and Geographical Phthisiology with special reference to the distribution of consumption in the United States, compiled and arranged in 1888 by George A. Evans, M. D., 909 Bedford Avenue, Brooklyn, N. Y., member of the Medical Society of the County of Kings, New York, member of the American Medical Association, and formerly Physician of the Atlantic Avenue and Bushwick and East Brooklyn Dispensaries, etc.

The showing for cities in the United States of deaths from consumption for each 10,000 of population is as follows:

New York, N. Y.	deaths per 10,000 inhabitants,	35.56
Philadelphia, Pa.	" " "	31.59
Brooklyn, N. Y.	" " "	29.84
Jersey City, N. J.	" " "	27.58
Paterson, N. J.	" " "	29.98
Baltimore, Md.	" " "	34.98
Washington, D. C.	" " "	41.96

Deaths per 1,000 inhabitants in New York State are as follows:

The State	deaths per 1,000 inhabitants,	2.5
New York City	" " "	3.5
Brooklyn	" " "	2.9
Richmond Co.	" " "	2.8
Suffolk Co.	" " "	2.0
Westchester Co.	" " "	2.0
Rockland Co.	" " "	1.9
Orange Co.	" " "	2.1
Ulster Co.	" " "	2.3
Greene Co.	" " "	2.7
SULLIVAN CO	" " "	**1.0**
DELAWARE CO	" " "	**1.2**
Otsego Co.	" " "	1.8
Broome Co.	" " "	2.1
Madison Co.	" " "	2.0
Oneida Co.	" " "	2.0
Oswego Co.	" " "	2.0
Saratoga Co.	" " "	2.6
Jefferson Co.	" " "	1.9
Warren Co.	" " "	1.6

Of the remaining counties Alleghany is the only one making as favorable a showing as Delaware. **Sullivan, with a percentage of 1.0, is the lowest in the State.** Dr. Evans makes the following note:

"The immediate neighborhood of Liberty, Sullivan Co., is one of the best regions, particularly during the summer and autumn months, within a 'day's journey' of New York City, for consumptives and others, who require a pure atmosphere with moderate elevation. This opinion is supported by statistics and by clinical experience."

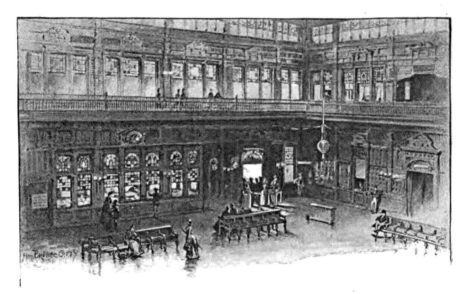

WEEHAWKEN PASSENGER STATION.

The following recommendation of Sullivan County, as a healthful as well as delightful summer home, is from the pen of Dr. Bronson, who ranks among the oldest and best practitioners of the city of Brooklyn:

"I take pleasure in recommending my patients to avail themselves of the pure and invigorating air of the country contiguous to Liberty, Sullivan Co. Many of them have gone to the resorts in the neighborhood and returned with new strength and vitality. My attention has been called to the White Sulphur Springs, situated four miles from the village, and an analysis of the mineral water carefully examined. I have no hesitation in indorsing the opinion of those who have been benefited by its use, and feel certain that it is an excellent help to those having kidney and similar diseases.

"To those in search of rest and recreation no pleasanter county can be chosen. The change from sea-coast humidity to clear and pure air produces immediately an improvement in general health. I have for years chosen those resorts on the line of the Ontario & Western Railway as a resting-place during my enforced vacations, and invariably return to practice in a refreshed condition of mind and body.

"The improved condition of the passenger accommodations on your line, noticed with pleasure on my recent trip to Oswego and return, will prove agreeable to the thousands who travel over it during the coming season.

"C. H. BRONSON, M. D.,
"438 Pacific Street.
"Brooklyn, March 1st, 1889."

Dr. Evans, of Brooklyn, writes:

"The statements concerning the healthfulness of Sullivan and Delaware counties, particularly the former, are substantiated by statistics, as any one may learn from the vital statistics of the census of 1880, and by my own experience (my patients are almost exclusively consumptives) and by that of my professional friends in this city; and, furthermore, I believe, and it is the consensus of the opinions of many prominent medical men who have given the 'climatic' treatment of consumptives careful study, that we have on the western slope of the Apalachian system (Sullivan and Delaware counties are the nearest points in the western slope of that system to New York City) climatic conditions, *throughout the whole year*, as good, if not superior to those on the eastern slope of the Cordilleran chain, *i. e.*, in Colorado, New Mexico, etc., so frequently resorted to by consumptives.

"G. A. EVANS,
"909 Bedford Avenue.
"Brooklyn, July 13th, 1889."

Dr. J. W. Van Dusen, Food Inspector, Department of Health, Brooklyn, writes:

"I have called on a number of farmers in the neighborhood of Liberty, Hurleyville, Woodbourne and Fallsburgh. I found the cattle in fine condition, being exclusively pasture and hay fed, producing as fine a quality of milk as is produced in the State. At the present time I have eleven children (young infants) in Sullivan County, and their progress is something remarkable. 1 must say that Sullivan County has all the elements to make it the most healthy summer resort in the East.

"J. W. VAN DUSEN, M. D.,
"901 Bedford Avenue.
"Brooklyn, August 9th, 1889."

Dr. Tracy, of New York, writes as follows:

"For several summers past, when opportunities offered, I have been in the habit of directing my patients to visit Sullivan County, N. Y. A person convalescent from a severe illness is in need, first of all, of pure air; other climatic conditions closely connected with air are temperature and humidity. In the neighborhood of Liberty, Sullivan Co., these conditions are well met. The moderate altitude gives a refreshing purity to a cool and bracing air, which especially during the last season proved most grateful to the invalid sent from this humid city. I have pleasure in cordially recommending this section to patient and 'summer home' seeker, and hoping that your efforts to bring before the public these advantages for health and recreation so near at hand may be appreciated, I am,

"Very truly yours,
"E. CLARK TRACY, M. D.,
"30 East 126th St.
"New York, January 29th, 1890."

Dr. Young writes:

"OFFICE OF THE COMMISSIONER OF HEALTH,
"Municipal Department Building,
"BROOKLYN, N. Y., March 9th, 1890.

"DEAR SIR: In answer to your circular received some time ago, desiring my views of Sullivan County as a summer resort, I most freely and willingly give expression to them in the following lines:

"My family have summered in many different places for several years past, but for the past five or six seasons they have settled down upon Monticello and the immediate vicinity as the place of all places for health and comfort, quiet and relaxation, fun and jollification, and for pleasure and sport of all kinds and varieties. The situation of Monticello, 1,560 feet above the level of the sea, is unsurpassed, if equaled, in any part of the State. The air is dry and bracing, cool and exhilarating; the water is pure, wholesome and plentiful; the scenery around and about it is grand and picturesque, variable and superb; the mosquito, that pest of many summer resorts, can find no abiding-place in it, and the place is seemingly free from all malarial influences. The ponds and lakes in the vicinity are large and numerous; the walks and drives are exceedingly pleasant, beautiful and romantic, and as the mountain roads are kept in good condition they are freely patronized.

"To sum up briefly, I would say that for invalids, and particularly those suffering from pulmonary troubles, no more health-restoring and fitting spot could be found than Sullivan County; for those desiring perfect rest and quiet, they can be enjoyed here to their fullest extent, and for those who seek relaxation from the ordinary routine of business, combined with rational pleasure and amusement, it will be found a very difficult task to select a more appropriate spot.

"I have thus given you, as briefly as possible, my views and opinions in answer to the circular addressed to me, but I think they are sufficiently explicit to convince you that I am an ardent admirer of Monticello and other beautiful spots in Sullivan County, both for their salubrity of climate and their health-restoring qualities.

"Respectfully,
"JOHN S. YOUNG, M. D.
"337 Bridge St., Brooklyn."

Rev. Dr. Bowdish writes:

"OLD JOHN ST. METHODIST EPISCOPAL CHURCH.

"I have been going with my family to the hills of Sullivan County for ten summers, each season with increasing satisfaction. Health and home are found in this section of the Empire State. There is no locality within the same distance of New York City where a person can get more for his money than in the vicinity of Liberty, Liberty Falls, Monticello and the surrounding country.

"The scenery along this route is exceedingly charming in its variety of mountain and meadow, river and lake. When any one has been privileged to spend the first summer pleasantly in this mountainous region, he contemplates the coming of the *second* season with restful delight. And when his second journey has actually begun, he can only dream of the welcome that awaits him in his summer home, and he commences already to feel the incoming of renewed strength to his wasted energies. Let me urge business men—bankers, brokers, merchants, mechanics and *ministers*, wearied in body and worried in mind, to halt. Rest, and try this trip. Get the health that will surely come to you in this mountain summerland.

"WELLESLEY W. BOWDISH, Pastor.
"Study, 44 John Street.
"NEW YORK, February 1st, 1890."

Dr. McLean writes:

"Dr. MALCOLM MCLEAN,
"29 East 126th Street,
"NEW YORK, March 20, 1890.

"DEAR SIR: It occurs to me that I may have neglected your communication of December 30th last, and will venture to say at this late day that I consider Sullivan County, in this State, a very healthful section, and should not hesitate to recommend it as a location for summer pilgrims.

"Yours very truly,
"MALCOLM MCLEAN, M. D."

Tent Life on the Delaware

Equipment.

ENGINES with extended smoke-box are used on all passenger trains, thereby avoiding the annoyance and discomfort of smoke and cinders. No cinders, no dust. Pullman Drawing-Room Cars are attached to all day trains. The additional rate for chairs from New York to all stations—Middletown to Parksville—is 50 cents; from Rockland to Apex, inclusive, 75 cents; from Walton to North Norwich, inclusive, $1.50; from Randallsville to Oneida, inclusive, $1.25; from North Bay to Oswego, $1.50. Night trains are equipped with Pullman Palace Buffet Sleeping Cars. The Sleeping Car rate, per double berth, from New York to Oneida and stations north, is $2.00; to points south of Oneida, $1.50. Reclining Chair Car free New York to Suspension Bridge on this train. The Day Coaches are models of beauty and comfort—mounted upon 42-inch paper wheels, the aisles carpeted, and the toilet-rooms in each car supplied with all the toilet requisites found on sleeping or parlor cars. The Day Express carries a special car devoted exclusively to ladies traveling alone or with their escorts. It is furnished with the Forney Car-seat, the latest and most improved seat in existence. The top of the seat is at a height which affords a support to the head, while the back inclines backward and has projections which support the lumbar regions of the spine where support is most needed to prevent fatigue while traveling.

To the Sportsman.

ALONG the Middle Division the country abounds in interest. The sportsman can find upon the hills and in the forests, in their season, quail, partridge, woodcock and snipe; and in the lakes of Sullivan and Delaware counties, and along the course of the East Branch, Little Delaware, Mongaup, Neversink and Susquehanna rivers, the red-head, buffle and woodduck, occasionally a canvas-back, while the "honk, honk" of the wild goose breaks the stillness of the early autumn air. Here, too, are found most of the four-footed game common to the more unfrequented portions of mountainous districts—rabbits, hares and squirrels.

But the trout-fishing in this region, among the crystal mountain streams, is a great attraction for the disciples of the gentle Izaak Walton. There are more than a hundred trout streams in Sullivan and Delaware, and a considerable number in Ulster, Chenango, Otsego, Madison and Oneida counties. They are annually visited by thousands of sportsmen, who take out by the hundreds these speckled beauties—the gamiest fish that swims. It would appear at first sight that the streams of Sullivan and Delaware would soon be "fished out," but the Company, with a desire to maintain their fishing qualities, have procured direct from the State Fish Hatchery, Caledonia Springs, N. Y., and from other parties since 1878, over seven million brook trout, besides a large number of lake and California trout. During 1892 one million brook trout were put in the trout streams from Walton to Mountain Dale, and this spring one million were again distributed in the same waters.

BROOK TROUT.

GENERAL description of the road has been given in the preceding pages. We now proceed to speak of the different stations along the line, specifying particularly those in which summer homes are offered. Crossing the Hudson river at the foot of West Forty-second or Franklin Streets, and entering the cars at Weehawken, one is whirled for the first fifty miles, with but few pauses, through a delightful suburban country, with its modern palatial residences and quaint old Dutch houses built with bricks brought from Holland centuries ago, and replete with romantic revolutionary and ante-revolutionary lore. The peaceful and fertile slopes of the valleys through which we pass have seen the course of carnage, the butchery of the tomahawk and bayonet, have echoed and re-echoed the bugles of conflicting armies, and under their carpet of green the bones of hundreds of combatants lie in unknown though honorable dust.

Probably few sections of our country contain so many scenes of beauty and points of historic interest as are found along the Hudson River Division of the road from Weehawken to Middletown, N. Y. The interest begins when first leaving the station at Weehawken, for one then passes almost over the spot where Alexander Hamilton and Aaron Burr fought their famous duel, the result of which threw a nation in mourning, and is increased as he reaches and glides swiftly past mountains, glens, islands and bays, where each one has furnished some legend that has made its name a household word in American homes. At Tappan, twenty miles from New York, the road skirts the base of the low hill upon the summit of which, in 1780, Major Andre was executed as a spy, and where his body remained until 1821. Seven miles north of Tappan the train plunges into the Haverstraw tunnel, and on emerging from the darkness far up on the mountain side one is greeted with a magnificent view. Below lies the broad Tappan Zee, dotted here and there with the white sails of river craft. Beyond, to the right, stretch the blue hills of Westchester County, while to the left can be seen the mountain ridges that mark the course of the lordly Hudson. A few miles beyond we pass Stony Point and enter the Highlands of the Hudson, whose scenery is unsurpassed by any in the world. This portion of the road is well known. Of its praises poets have sung and historians have written, and anything of an attempt towards its description, in such a work as this, would be unwelcome. Justly celebrated has it been from the time when Hendrick Hudson and his adventuresome crew gazed upon the shores from the deck of the "Half Moon." A well-known writer says: "The Danube has, in part, glimpses of such grandeur; the Elbe has sometimes such delicately penciled effects; but no European river is so lordly in its bearing; none flows in such grandeur to the sea." The roadway, following closely the edge of the river, is hewn out of the solid rock that forms the base of the Dunderberg, Crow's Nest and Storm King Mountains. These, together with Anthony's Nose, opposite, form the highest of the Highland group, their summits rising 1,200 feet above the water. Gloomy and grand they stand in all their massive proportions, with scarred and rugged battlements, against which the storms of ages have beaten, arousing in the mind of the beholder an overpowering sense of nature's majesty.

Rapidly passing the United States Military Academy at West Point, we reach Cornwall.

From the Hudson to the Wallkill.

Leaving the Hudson at Cornwall, the road climbs the hills in its passage across the County of Orange, the first station being

WEST CORNWALL, ORANGE CO.

The railroad station for Cornwall and Cornwall-on-the-Hudson. This locality has long been popular as a summer resort. Charmingly situated on the hill-side, overlooking some beautiful river scenery, with a resident population of about 1,000 inhabitants. There are here several large hotels and boarding-houses for the accommodation of summer guests.

Cornwall has recently been incorporated. The streets are now lighted at night and watered in dusty weather. There are many attractive drives in and around Cornwall—the one to West Point being probably the favorite.

56 MILES FROM NEW YORK.
FARE, $1.08;
EXCURSION, $2.00.

CORNWALL MOUNTAIN HOUSE.

WEST CORNWALL STATION—Cornwall-on-Hudson Post-Office.

J. W. MEAGHER—Mountain House. The house is 1½ miles from the river, at an elevation of 1,200 feet, on the western slope of the famous Storm King Mountain, commanding a river and landscape view not surpassed in this country for beauty and extent; air pure and dry; nights cool; malaria and mosquitoes unknown; house supplied with water from artesian wells; among the many attractions of interest are a dancing-pavilion, new bowling-alley, billiard-parlor and lawn tennis grounds; table and appointments not excelled; abundance of fresh vegetables from our own place; electric bells in every room; access from New York by N. Y., O. & W. R'y; stages and buckboards will meet trains when advised; accommodate 200; rates on application; transient $3.50; discount to season guests; first-class livery. Write for circular.

Mrs. C. B. MARTIN—Select family hotel. ½ mile; accommodate 75; adults $6 to $10, transient $1.50, children special; broad piazza; extensive, well-shaded grounds; near post-office; raise own vegetables; convenient to church. References and circulars on application.

Miss MARY C. CLARK—Woodbine Cottage. ¼ mile; accommodate 5; adults $6, transient $1.

Mr. SOUTHWELL—Near station; accommodate 10; adults $6, children $3.

Miss H. M. HAMILTON (Cornwall Post-Office)—Farm-house. 1½ miles; accommodate 12; adults $7 to $8, children $3 to $5, transient $1.50; a country house located on main road, very pleasant and desirable, convenient to post-office and church; ample shade; excellent livery; large rooms. References on application.

CATHERINE E. SMITH (Cornwall Post-Office)—Boarding-house. 1½ miles; accommodate 25; adults $7 to $10, children $4 to $6, transient $1.50.

ABRAM S. CLARK (Cornwall Landing Post-Office)—Prospect House. Accommodate 14; adults $7 to $8, children half price, transient 50 cents per meal.

ORR'S MILLS, ORANGE CO.

Four miles from Cornwall the roadway crosses Moodna Creek by an iron bridge 1,100 feet long and 105 feet above the water, giving a beautiful bird's-eye view of the country. At the western end of the bridge is the station, and within a stone's throw of it is located the Moodna Mansion—William Orr, Proprietor. The house is situated upon elevated ground, commanding picturesque views of the surrounding country, and is replete with all modern improvements, including gas.

57 MILES FROM NEW YORK. FARE, $1.08; EXCURSION, $2.00.

ORR'S MILLS STATION—Orr's Mills Post-Office.

WILLIAM ORR—Moodna Mansion. At depot; accommodate 40; adults $7 to $10, reduction for children, transient $1.50 to $2; discount to season guests; situated on a knoll in view of Moodna river; large lawn; finest forest shade trees; spacious grounds for outdoor amusement; all modern improvements, including gas, water, etc.; raise our own vegetables; good gunning and fishing; first-class livery; house stands on historic ground, famous for Revolutionary scenes. This is the 25th year that Mr. and Mrs. Orr will entertain guests, and their experience and ways have made many friends for them. The Moodna Mansion will be a very desirable place for any that might desire to stop off on their way back to the city, and will offer special prices for September. References exchanged.

Mrs. A. A. RYDER—Boarding and farm-house. Near station; accommodate 25; adults $6 to $8, children half price.

MEADOW BROOK, ORANGE CO.

Situated two miles back from the Hudson and several hundred feet above it. Overlooking both mountain and river scenery, and surrounded by a rich agricultural district.

58 MILES FROM NEW YORK. FARE, $1.26; EXCURSION, $2.10.

MEADOW BROOK STATION—Meadow Brook Post-Office.

Mrs. M. A. COOPER—Farm-house. Station on farm; accommodate 12; adults $5 to $6, children half price; have a large shady lawn; plenty of milk, fresh eggs and vegetables; our motto is to please; good table; healthy location. References on application.

Mrs. G. H. Moore—Farm-house. 2 miles; accommodate 12; 5 rooms; adults $5 to $6, children $2 to $4, transient $1; delightfully situated; large rooms; fine lawn; music; croquet; good water; raise our own vegetables; will endeavor to please. Address Post-office Box 122, Newburgh, N. Y.

E. S. Benedict—Accommodate 15; adults $6, children $3.

GENUNG'S, Orange Co.

61 MILES FROM NEW YORK. LOCAL FARE, $1.35; EXCURSION, $2.20.

Near this station was the place of encampment of the Revolutionary Army during two long winters, and from the car windows can be seen the headquarters of Generals Knox and Reed.

GENUNG'S STATION—Little Britain Post-Office.

Mrs. V. F. Knapp—Large farm-house. 1½ miles; accommodate 15; adults $5 to $6, children according to age, transient $1.25; free transportation; raise our own vegetables; abundance of milk, eggs, etc.; beautiful views; swinging hammocks; piano, etc.; pleasant drives; convenient to the city of Newburgh, where Washington's headquarters and other places of note may be found; good fishing; summer and winter boarders; convenient to church and post-office; boats at a reasonable rate. References on application.

Mrs. H. Coleman—Oak Ridge Farm. ¼ mile; accommodate 10; 9 rooms; adults $5 to $6, transient $1; no small children or Hebrews taken; free transportation; raise our own vegetables; good fishing and gunning; livery on place; ½ mile to church and post-office; fine mountain scenery; no malaria; 450 feet above Hudson; plenty of shade; large piazza; music; abundance of fresh eggs, milk and poultry; summer and winter boarders. Refers to Miss Alice F. Hotchkiss, 256 Rodney Street, Brooklyn, E. D.; R. Phillips, 363 Tompkins Avenue, Brooklyn; Marvin A. D. Harris, 47 Broad Street, N. Y.

R. W. Genung—Modern farm house. 3 minutes' walk from depot; accommodate 10; terms $7 to $10, transient and children not taken; piano; well-kept hady grounds; horses and carriages; beautiful drives in all directions. References and full particulars on application.

Curtis M. Nixon—Farm-house. 2 miles; accommodate 12; adults $7, children according to age, no transient taken; large and shady lawn; good table; free transportation; raise own vegetables; 1 mile from church; pleasant walks and drives; good running spring water. References exchanged.

A. C. Howell—Farm-house. 1½ miles; accommodate 20; adults $7, children $3 to $5.

Mrs. M. C. Finley—Accommodate 20; adults $5 to $7, children half price. Write for particulars.

John A. Clark—Farm-house. 4 miles; accommodate 14; adults $6, children $3, transient $1.50. Post-office Box 188, Newburgh, N. Y.

ROCK TAVERN, Orange Co.

68 MILES FROM NEW YORK. LOCAL FARE, $1.47; EXCURSION, $2.36.

An important locality in the old days of the stage coach, situated in a farming region famous for its fertility.

ROCK TAVERN STATION—Coldenham Post-Office.

Mrs. Samuel Arnott—Sunset Farm. 4 miles; accommodate 10; adults $6 to $8, children $4, discount to season guests; situated on high ground; beautifully shaded; elevation 700 feet above the Hudson; we have a dairy of cows affording the best milk and butter; raise own vegetables; plenty of eggs; transportation 50 cents. Refers to H. G. Disbrow, 58 Warren Street, N. Y.; Mrs. King, 134 W. 130th Street, New York.

BURNSIDE, ORANGE CO.

Surrounded with fields of green and gold, with fertile valleys watered with crystal streams running through wide-spread meadows.

66 MILES FROM NEW YORK.
LOCAL FARE, $1.60;
EXCURSION, $2.46.

CAMPBELL HALL, ORANGE CO.

The junction point with the Wallkill Valley, Central New England & Western, Pennsylvania, Poughkeepsie & Boston and Orange County Railroads. It is surrounded with the broad and fertile farms for which Orange County is famous.

66 MILES FROM NEW YORK.
FARE, $1.66;
EXCURSION, $2.95.

CAMPBELL HALL STATION—Campbell Hall Post-Office.

Mrs. S. S. HALL—Boarding-house. Near station; accommodate 15. Terms on application.
HAMLIN JONES—Farm-house. 1¼ miles; accommodate 7; adults $7, children $4.50.
DANIEL DALY—Hotel and boarding-house. At station; accommodate 25; adults $7, children $3.50, transient $2.

ORANGE COUNTY STOCK.

Wallkill Valley Railroad.

Connections are made at Campbell Hall with the Wallkill Valley Railroad, making not only the shortest but the most attractive route from New York to all the summer resorts on and adjacent to this line. For its entire length the route runs through the valley of the Wallkill. To the northwest, far as the eye can reach, stretched the Shawangunk Mountains, while to the southeast, like piled-up walls of azure, lie the range of hills shutting in the Hudson river. No lovelier country can be found than that lying in this valley. In whatever direction one turns, his eye is greeted and his senses freshened with the sight of the grazing and dairy farms, with their fields of waving grain and grass, dotted here and there with herds of lowing cattle, with spacious barns, filled to overflowing with the fruits of careful husbandry, bearing witness to the prosperity of the land.

MONTGOMERY, ORANGE CO.

A quiet hamlet on the Wallkill river, with 1,200 inhabitants. It has good hotels, where the comfort of summer visitors is looked after and their wants supplied. The bass-fishing in the river is excellent.

75 MILES FROM NEW YORK.
FARE, $1.71;
EXCURSION, $2.60.

MONTGOMERY STATION – Montgomery Post-Office.

Mrs. A. Bryson—River View Farm House. 10 minutes' drive; accommodate 20; rates on application; transient $1; house situated on hill, affording a magnificent view of the surrounding country; river flowing near by; large shady yard; unusually good churches within a short walk; occasional drives free; raise own vegetables; excellent fishing and gunning; good livery attached. References on application.

John J. Crawford—Farm-house. 2½ miles; accommodate 12; adults $6, children $4; discount to season guests; free transportation; raise our own vegetables; good bass and pickerel fishing in Wallkill river; free boats and fishing-tackle to guests; 2½ miles from church. Refers to Station Agent and also to Postmaster, Montgomery, N. Y.

William F. Draper—Farm-house. 3 miles; accommodate 14; adults $7, children $4, transient $1; table supplied with the best vegetables, eggs, and milk from our own place; healthy location; pure spring water; stabling for horses; good bass and pickerel fishing; free transportation; discount to season guests. Refers to C. H. Hammer, 2029 Brandywine Street, Philadelphia, Pa.; Frank Fulton, Monticello, N. Y.

P. O. Box 256, Montgomery, N. Y.—Private house. Near the Wallkill river; ⅛ mile; 6 large pleasant rooms; adults $5, transient $1; families wishing unfurnished apartments for boarding themselves can be accommodated at reasonable rates.

Mrs. HARRISON SMITH—Private residence. ¼ mile; accommodate 6; adults $5 to $6, children $3 to $4.

Mrs. L. S. BROWN—Elmwood Farm House. ½ mile; accommodate 10; adults $6 to $7, transient $1; discount to season guests.

THEODORE LEAVENWORTH—Farm Cottage. 3 miles; accommodate 8; adults $5, children $2 to $4, transient $1.

J. J. VAN KEUREN—Meadow View Farm House. 1 mile; accommodate 15; adults $5 to $7, children $3.50.

ABNER SHAFER—Farm-house. 3 miles; accommodate 12; terms moderate.

A. REYNOLDS—Riverside Farm House. Accommodate 18; adults $6; no Hebrews taken.

E. VAN WAGNER—Hotel. ¼ mile; accommodate 50; adults $5 to $12, transient $2. Send for circular.

WALDEN, ORANGE CO.,

Is an enterprising and thrifty village, situated in the extreme northern part of the county, within the limits of the town of Montgomery, surrounded by charming pastoral estates, many of them the country residence of New York City's well-to-do merchants. From this point may be seen the highest peaks of the Catskills, while the glittering white of the Shawangunk range is brought to vivid view from reflections of the rising sun. Mohonk and Minnewaska are but a short distance, to which points many picnic parties resort from here.

[70 MILES FROM NEW YORK. FARE $1.62; EXCURSION, $3.02.]

Within the village are many handsome residences, while its active 3,000 population support three churches, two banks and two weekly papers of large circulation. Its educational facilities are of the best High-School order, carried on within a splendid new school-house that cost over $10,000. It contains also two of the largest cutlery establishments in the country, besides a woolen-mill, knitting-mill, overall factory, and the Rider Engine Works, where hot-air pumping engines are made.

Walden is a healthful summer resort for such as desire to get out of the city, and still be near, for it is only a short three hours' ride from New York, and should receive a wider recognition.

WALDEN STATION—Walden Post-Office.

DAVID STEWART—Private house. 10 minutes' walk; accommodate 12; adults $4 to $7, children $3, transient $1; omnibus transportation 10 cents; excellent fishing; good livery; church near by; good table; pleasant walks and drives. References and full particulars on application.

R. W. CORSA—Farm-house. ¼ mile; accommodate 10; adults $6 to $7.

J. R. McVAY—Farm-house. ½ mile; rates and full particulars on application.

C. VAN ZANDT—Lakeside House. 5 miles; terms and circulars on application.

C. E. WHIGAM—Whigam Dale Farm. Accommodate 40; adults $7 to $10, children $5.

WALLKILL, ULSTER CO.

62 MILES FROM NEW YORK.
FARE, $1.92;
EXCURSION, $3.22.

The next station is a small village of about 600 inhabitants, surrounded by beautiful agricultural and grazing lands. One mile south of the village is located the factory of the New York Condensed Milk Company, J. J. Borden, Manager. During the summer they receive and condense as high as 30,000 quarts of milk per day, employing about 100 hands. A visit to the factory would well repay one for the time. The whole establishment bears testimony to the belief in the motto that "cleanliness is next to godliness." Not a speck of dirt can be found inside the building.

WALLKILL STATION—Wallkill Post-Office.

PETER WHITE—Farm-house. 2 miles; accommodate 30; abundance of fresh milk, butter and eggs; situated on high ground, affording a magnificent view of Lake Mohonk and surrounding country; three piazzas; plenty of shade; raise own vegetables; free transportation; 1 mile from church. Rates and references on application.

Mrs. L. B. DEYO—Private boarding-house. ½ mile; accommodate 6; adults $5 to $6, children $3; situated in a fine farming country and accessible to Lakes Mohonk and Minnewaska, either by rail or carriage. Refers to Mr. Oliver Johnston, Johnston Bros., corner Fulton Street and Flatbush Avenue, Brooklyn, N. Y.

WALLKILL STATION—Galeville Mills Post-Office.

D. W. HASBROUCK—Farm-house. 2½ miles; accommodate 40; special rates for fall and winter guests; rates on application and according to rooms; separate rooms for each person; transportation 25 cents; brick house with inside blinds; house situated on a hill, and grounds extend to the Wallkill river; plenty of boats; excellent shade; summer seats and hammocks; 100 feet of piazza; organ and new piano; livery, and accommodations for those wishing to bring their own horses and carriages; convenient to Lakes Mohonk and Minnewaska; good fishing; plenty of fresh milk, eggs, butter, ice-cream, chickens and ducks; 1½ miles from churches. References on application; house opens on May 28th.

W. J. MERRITT—Farm-house. 2 miles; accommodate 20; large piazza; plenty of shade; convenient to Lakes Mohonk and Minnewaska; abundance of fresh milk, butter and eggs; raise own vegetables; excellent fishing; first-class livery. Rates and references on application.

W. H. DECKER (Bruynsuick Post-Office)—Brookside Farm. 6 miles; accommodate 24; terms and full particulars on application.

GARDINER, ULSTER CO.

66 MILES FROM NEW YORK.
FARE $2.09;
EXCURSION, $3.56.

Gardiner is a thriving little village of probably 200 inhabitants, and is pleasantly situated in the Wallkill Valley—one of the most beautiful valleys in the entire State. To the west of the village, and less than half a mile from it, is the Wallkill river, which abounds in black-bass and other good fishing. The location is perfectly healthy, the village being only about four miles on an air line from the grand old Shawangunk Mountains. A number of farm-houses in the vicinity will accommodate city people with board.

GARDINER STATION—Gardiner Post-Office.

Mrs. LUTHER SEYMOUR—Fair View Farm. 3 miles; accommodate 8; beautiful mountain scenery; raise own vegetables; discount to season guests; excellent fishing; free transportation; adults preferred; no Jews wanted. Rates and full particulars on application.

ABRAM LINDERBECK—Accommodate 8; adults $6. Write for particu ars.

EDWARD MITCHELL—Farm-house. 2 miles; accommodate 8; adults $5; young people preferred.

GARDINER STATION—Rutsonville Post-Office.

T. C. EDMUNDS—Farm-house, Rutson. 4 miles; accommodate 30; adults $5 to $7, children $3 under 12 years, transient reasonable rates; discount to season guests; transportation 50 cents; large farm-house; two piazzas in front and back; a lake near the house; a splendid view of mountains 5,000 feet high; healthy climate; no mosquitoes or malaria; abundance of fruit of all kinds; plenty of eggs and milk; good fishing and gunning; first-class livery; 2½ miles to church. Refers to Wm. T. and E. E. Wallace, Pine Bush, N. Y.; Taylor & Howell, Pine Bush, N. Y., and Wm. S. Martin, Dwaarskill, N. Y.

GARDINER STATION—Modena Post-Office.

H. MINARD—Farm-house. 4 miles; accommodate 20; adults $6; elevation 1,200 feet, commanding a fine view of over 100 miles of the Catskill and Shawangunk Mountains; well-shaded yards; fine walks and drives; all kinds of fruit; vegetables; plenty of milk, eggs and butter. Refers to Dr. A. Birdsall, 546 Bedford Avenue, Brooklyn, N. Y.; J. F. Roberts, 268 Keap Street, Brooklyn, N. Y.; C. H. Sibbald, 387 Halsey Street, Brooklyn, N. Y., and J. McCollum, 222 4th Street, Jersey City, N. J.

ELI WAUP (Plattskill Post-Office)—Farm-house. Accommodate 10; adults $6.

NEW PALTZ, ULSTER CO.

A very thrifty village of 850 inhabitants, with three churches, two banks, two weekly newspapers, and a State Normal School with a large attendance.

| 93 MILES FROM NEW YORK. |
| FARE, $2.21; |
| EXCURSION, $3.65. |

New Paltz is the railroad station of Lake Mohonk and Lake Minnewaska mountain houses. New Paltz has had an extraordinary growth of late, the population having increased fifty per cent. in five years. The village has been incorporated and the streets generally graveled, provided with street lamps and flagging-stone sidewalks. The houses erected during the past five years are occupied, to a great extent, by people desiring the advantages of a first-class education for their children at the State Normal and Training School, of which Dr. F. S. Cohen is Principal. The library advantages of New Paltz, coupled with the prevailing low rates of taxation and the almost entire absence of the rough element, makes this village a particularly desirable residence for people of means and culture.

NEW PALTZ STATION—New Paltz Post-Office.

Mrs. PERRY DEYO—Farm-house. 1 mile; accommodate 20; adults $6, children over 10 full price, transient $1.50. It is only a few minutes' walk to the river, where good bathing and boating can be obtained; fine shady lawn for croquet and tennis; plenty of swings; 4 miles to Lakes Mohonk and Minnewaska hotels; large piazza; fine drives in all directions; scenery unsurpassed; raise own vegetables; good fishing and gunning; boats free to guests; free transportation. Refers to Mrs. James Hall, 363 W. 15th Street, New York; W. E. DuBois, 453 7th Street, Brooklyn, N. Y.

NEW PALTZ STATION—Mohonk Lake Post-Office.

J. IRVING GODDARD—Mountain Rest Boarding-house. 4 miles; accommodate 40; adults $9 to $16, transient $2; transportation $1; situated in the centre of the Mohonk estate, all its attractions, including 40 miles of drives, are open to guests of Mountain Rest; altitude 1,200 feet; extensive views of the Wallkill and the Rondout Valleys and the Catskill Mountains. Apply for circular.

NEW PALTZ STATION—Springtown Post-Office.

Mrs. JAMES DEYO—Farm-house. 1½ miles; accommodate 25; adults $6, transient $1; Wallkill river a few yards from the house, affording good boating and fishing; short drive to Lake Mohonk; boats free to guests; excellent fishing; raise own vegetables; very good gunning; first-class table, supplied with the best of milk and eggs from the farm; free transportation; large shady lawn; good spring water; five minutes' walk to all churches. Opens June 15th; references on application.

SIMON R. LeFEVER—Farm-house. ½ mile; accommodate 15; adults $6, children $3, transient $1; discount to season guests; ¼ mile to Wallkill river; grand scenery of the Shawangunk Mountains; short distance from Lakes Mohonk and Minnewaska; boats free; raise own vegetables; free transportation. Refers to Jesse Eltinge, P.M., New Paltz, N. Y.

GEORGE K. McMURDY—River View Cottage. ¼ mile; accommodate 20; adults $6 to $8, children on application, transient $1.50; discount to season guests; situated on high ground, commanding fine views of the Catskill and Shawangunk Mountains; plenty of shade; pleasant walks; abundance of vegetables, eggs, butter and milk, fresh from the farm. References on application.

Mrs. E. H. HUTCHINSON (New Paltz Post-Office)—Private residence. On hill; accommodate 8; adults $5 to $6; no small children.

LAKE MOHONK

Is located near the summit of Sky-Top, one of the highest of the Shawangunk Mountains, in Ulster County, and is about five miles from New Paltz Station, to which point the hotel stages run, meeting every train.

> 95 MILES FROM NEW YORK.
> FARE, INCLUDING STAGE, $3.45;
> EXCURSION, $6.40.

All who visit the lake are impressed with the wonderful and greatly varied character of the scenery—a beautiful lake; massive rocks, each of them thousands of tons in weight; towering cliffs and far-extended views in all directions, embracing large portions of six States, and covering several thousand square miles. A well-known writer says: "One of those rare places where the creative power seems to have rehearsed for every form of grandeur and gentleness; an Alpine lake on the top of a mountain, 1,200 feet above the valley, the mountain itself a gigantic monument of rock scenery wrought into every form of wildness and grace, and from any point on the summit cliffs an outlook over two perfect valleys, with fifty miles of the western horizon crowded with glorious mountain ranges, amid whose mysterious realms the sinking sun and the mountain mist work such magic as only poetry exalted to worship can fitly rehearse." The Mohonk House is located on the edge of the lake, and commands a magnificent view of lake and mountain. The rear of the hotel looks out upon the extensive Rondout Valley, bounded by the

LAKE MOHONK.

Shandaken Mountains and some of the Catskills on the north. Adjacent to the hotel the grounds have been graded and smoothed and converted into handsome lawns, interspersed with native trees, under whose shade the huge rocks form seats of every imaginable shape and character. The proprietors have constructed walks and stairs, rustic arbors, seats and bridges, with skill and taste. Names have easily been attached to these romantic walks, so that days and weeks are pleasantly spent in exploring them.

The season opens June 1st and closes October 20th to November 1st. Communications in regard to board, rooms, etc., should be addressed to the proprietor, Albert K. Smiley, Mohonk, Ulster County, New York.

NEW PALTZ STATION—Mohonk Lake Post-Office.

ALBERT K. SMILEY—Lake Mohonk Mountain House. 6 miles: accommodate 300: transportation $1.25 each way, trunk 50 cents. Please write for circulars giving full description, terms, references, etc.

LAKE MINNEWASKA

Is located on the summit of the Shawangunk Mountains, ten miles southwest of New Paltz. The lake is much larger than Mohonk, and is surrounded by the same extraordinary bluffs and masses of tumbled rocks. A writer in the New York *Evening Mail* thus describes the lake:

103 MILES FROM NEW YORK.
FARE, INCLUDING STAGE, $3.71;
EXCURSION, $6.00.

"Set into the hills like a bowl is the beautiful Lake Minnewaska, flanked on one side and end by bold, precipitous cliffs, and on the other side and end by sloping wooded shores. Along these cliffs and shores, both at their summits and low down by the edge of the lake, are walks conveniently cleared of undergrowth and provided at frequent intervals with rustic, thatch-roofed kiosks or summer houses, offering most inviting spots for rest. No summer resort anywhere is more amply provided with attractive strolls and with seats. Minnewaska Lake is noticeable for the magnificent broken bluffs at its eastern borders."

The Minnewaska Mountain House was opened in 1879. It is located on Minnewaska Heights, 150 feet above the lake, and about 1,800 feet above tide-water, or nearly as high as the Catskill Mountain House, and from every room in the hotel there are magnificent valley and mountain views, taking in the mountains of New Jersey on the south, the Highlands of the Hudson and Newburgh Bay on the southeast, the Housatonic Mountains of Connecticut to the east, the whole line of the Berkshire Mountains of Massachusetts and the Green Mountains of Vermont to the northeast, the Helderberg Mountains

LAKE MINNEWASKA.

to the north, the bold outlines of the Catskills and the Shandaken Mountains to the northwest, and the Neversink and Shawangunk hills to the southwest. The views embrace several river valleys, including the valley of the Hudson from Cornwall to the mountains about Lake George.

All communications regarding rooms and board should be addressed to the proprietor, Mr. Alfred H. Smiley, Minnewaska, Ulster County, N. Y.

ROSENDALE, ULSTER CO.

The village proper has a population of about 1,000 inhabitants. The principal industry is the manufacture of the famous "Rosendale Cement," the daily output of which, over the whole district, reaches about 9,000 barrels. At Rosendale the roadway crosses the Rondout Creek and D. & H. Canal by an iron bridge 150 feet high and 960 feet long, giving a glorious bird's-eye view of the valleys on both sides. From the bridge the cement quarries, in the perpendicular face of the mountains, look like the caves of the ancient cliff dwellers.

100 MILES FROM NEW YORK.
FARE, $2.40;
EXCURSION, $4.30.

ROSENDALE STATION—Rosendale Post-Office.

Mrs. L. B. ROOSA—Farm-house. ¼ mile; accommodate 15; adults $5 to $6, children $3, transient $1.

J. H. BAKER (Leibhardt Post-Office)—Farm-house. 10 miles; accommodate 20; adults $4 to $5, children half.

CHARLES V. TERWILLIGER (Binnewater Station, Accord Post-Office)—Farm-house. Adults $6; families desired.

WHITEPORT STATION—Whiteport Post-Office.

Mrs. P. RYAN—Farm-house. ¼ mile; accommodate 14; ladies $5, gentlemen $6, children according to age; free transportation; a pleasantly situated house; on high ground; very healthy; within five minutes' walk of grove and woodland; raise our own vegetables; excellent fishing and gunning; livery accommodation; churches of various denominations within 1 mile of house; first-class table, well supplied from products of farm; pleasant rooms; ample shade; Wallkill Valley R.R. passes within 200 yards of house. Refers to F. Doremus, Superintendent Newark & Rosendale Cement Co., Whiteport, N. Y., and Dr. Chispell, Rondout, N. Y. Further particulars on application.

Central New England & Western R.R.

Connection, in Union Station, is made at Campbell Hall with trains of the C. N. E. & W. Railroad—" the Poughkeepsie Bridge Route "—running northeasterly across Orange County to the Hudson at Highland, and crossing the river at that point to Poughkeepsie on a magnificent bridge 175 feet above the water and 3,093 feet long. A magnificent bird's-eye view can be had of the Hudson river both north and south from the car windows while crossing the bridge. The C. N. E. & W. Railroad makes direct connections in Union Stations at Canaan with trains of the Housatonic Railroad for points in the Berkshire Hills, and at Hartford with trains for Boston.

CLINTONDALE, ULSTER CO.,

On the main line of the Central New England & Western Railroad, twenty miles east of Campbell Hall, is a thriving village situated on the western slope of a range of hills overlooking the great Wallkill Valley, with the Shawangunk Mountains in the background. The location is perfectly healthy, and a large number of summer boarders are accommodated at this place.

| FARE, $2.11; |
| EXCURSION, $3.06. |

CLINTONDALE STATION—Clintondale Post-Office.

S. BAKER—Farm-house. 2 miles; accommodate 20; adults $6, children $3 to $4, transient $1; discount to guests remaining six weeks or more; raise own vegetables; excellent fishing and gunning; transportation charges 25 cents; first-class table; picturesque views. References on application.

S. P. THORN—Locust Farm House. ¼ mile; accommodate 45; adults $7 to $9, children under ten $5, transient $1.50; locality is considered by all who have visited it once as being the most healthful; magnificent views of the surrounding country; excellent gunning and fishing; within ¼ mile of all churches; raise own vegetables; transportation charges 25 cents; first-class table, supplied with abundance of milk, butter and eggs, and fruits of all kinds. For further particulars and references apply as above; for circulars apply to J. S. Eakins, 24 Liberty Street, New York.

O. T. D.NGER—Farm-house. 2 miles; accommodate 25; adults $5 to $6, children $4 to $5, transient $1; situated on high ground, commanding a magnificent view of the surrounding country; good table; fresh butter, eggs, poultry and fruit; transportation charges 25 cents; 12 large spacious rooms; ¼ mile from church. References on application.

E. S. ANDREWS—Fruit Farm Villa. Near station; accommodate 20? rates and particulars on application.

HIGHLAND STATION—Highland Post-Office.

N. H. ZIMMERMAN—Elm Cottage. 1¼ miles; accommodate 20; terms and full particulars on application.

Across Orange County.

STONY FORD, Orange Co.

Leaving Campbell Hall, the first station in Stony Ford, lying amid those well-tilled Orange County farms, with their general aspect of thrift and prosperity, betokening an energy on the part of the inhabitants looking to the best possible use of the gifts which nature has bestowed upon them. Mr. Charles Backman's famous stock farm is located here, and on it have been raised some of the most celebrated trotting horses in this country.

FARE, $1.65;
EXCURSION, $2.00.

STONY FORD STATION—Stony Ford Post-Office.

Miss FANNIE MILLER—Farm-house. 1 mile; accommodate 10; adults $5.50 to $6, children on application, transient $1; house situated on slight elevation; light, pleasant rooms; well-shaded lawn; good livery at reasonable rates; fine roads for bicycle riding; raise own vegetables. References on application.

Mrs. J. C. WILBER—Farm-house. Accommodate 12; adults $6 to $7; pleasant and healthy location; liberal table; boating and tennis; livery and accommodation for horses at reasonable rates; situated in the famous Wallkill Valley; picturesque scenery. References on application.

Mrs. E. H. CRAWFORD—Farm-house. 1 mile; accommodate 10; adults $5 to $7, rates for children on application; large and airy rooms; abundance of shade; daily mail; raise own vegetables; free transportation; good fishing; situated near the Wallkill river. References on application.

THOMAS S. FARREY—La Grange Hotel. Accommodate 10; adults $5.

CRYSTAL RUN, Orange Co.

Situated in one of the finest farming sections of the well-known County of Orange. The air is healthful and bracing. Between Crystal Run and Stony Ford runs a small stream of pure crystal water, from which the place derives its name. The Wallkill river, with a splendid sandy bottom, is within one-quarter mile of the station, and affords fine bass-fishing as well as boating and bathing. The roads around Crystal Run are magnificent.

FARE, $1.65;
EXCURSION, $2.70.

CRYSTAL RUN STATION—Crystal Run Post-Office.

Mrs. M. J. STAGE—Farm-house. 1 mile; accommodate 15; rates and references on application; plenty of shade; abundance of fresh milk, eggs, butter and fruit; raise own vegetables; excellent fishing and gunning; free transportation.

Mrs. ANDREW CRANS—Farm-house. Station on farm; accommodate 20; adults $6 to $10, children $2 to $4; free transportation; Wallkill river runs through farm; good boating and fishing; raise our own vegetables; 2 miles to church. References on application.

Mrs. MARTIN VANDEWATER—Farm-house. 1 mile; accommodate 10; adults $8, children $4, transient $1.50; abundance of fresh vegetables, poultry, eggs, butter and fruit; bath-room; pleasant drives; plenty of shade; swings and hammocks; very healthy location; raise own vegetables; first-class livery; free transportation. Refers to J. L. Wiggins, Middletown, N. Y.; F. C. Vandewater, Hawthorne Street, Flatbush, N. Y.

Mrs. GEORGE J. HOUSTON—Farm-house. 2 miles; accommodate 10; adults $5 to $6, children $3 to $4, transient $1.

WALLKILL RIVER.

MECHANICSTOWN, ORANGE CO.

Situated four miles from Goshen, the county seat of Orange County, and two and a half miles from the city of Middletown, with post-office, telegraph and express office. The Wallkill river, whose waters teem with the gamy bass and pickerel, runs within a half mile of the station. Good woodcock and quail shooting; boating, bathing; good livery and fine roads. A large hotel, located on the shore of the river, and several commodious farm-houses will accommodate those who wish to avail themselves of the privileges of much larger places at lower rates.

78 MILES FROM NEW YORK.
FARE, $1.68;
EXCURSION, $2.75.

MIDDLETOWN, ORANGE CO.,

Next to Newburgh the largest town in Orange Co., and situated

| 70 MILES FROM NEW YORK.
| FARE, $1.00;
| EXCURSION, $2.75. |

545 feet above tide-water, was made a city by Act of the Legislature, taking effect June 30th, 1888. The census of 1870 gave a population of 8,494, while 1890 gives 11,918, a gain of over forty per cent., a rate of increase equaled by no city or village in southern New York. The city is beautifully located in the midst of a fine agricultural district, and is the centre of trade for a large part of Orange, Sullivan and Delaware counties. The trade of the young city is growing more and more extensive each year, and with reason, for its stores of every kind are as large and as well stocked as those usually found in cities with many times the population. On the western outskirts of the city, in the midst of spacious and well-kept grounds, is the New York State Homœopathic Hospital for the Insane. The buildings provide for about 600 patients, and the accommodations are now taxed to their fullest capacity. The hospital buildings were erected at a cost of a trifle more than $1,000,000, and in addition to this a very considerable sum has been expended in adorning and beautifying the grounds, free access to which is given.

Middletown has ten churches, two national banks, and a savings and private bank; two daily, two semi-weekly and two weekly papers. Its principal manufacturing industries are saws, files, wool and straw hats and the finer grades of leather. The city is growing steadily in favor as a place of residence, many wealthy families being attracted to it by its fine schools, broad, well-shaded and well-kept streets, its abundant water-supply and its refined and cultured society. The city has a number of well-kept hotels, and in and about it are a number of families who will receive summer boarders. In the Wallkill river, but a few miles away, and in Monhagen Lake, but a mile from the city limits, fine bass and pickerel fishing may be enjoyed. At Wickham Avenue Station, Middletown, is located a large and attractive dining-room, where the famous Orange County milk and butter, beside other wholesome food, is served in abundance; brook trout and game served in season. The restaurant is run by Wm. Seeholzer. All trains stop for meals.

MIDDLETOWN STATION—Middletown Post-Office.

JOHN K. MOFFET—"The Moffet" Boarding-house. Accommodate 25; adults $7 to $10, transient $1.50; raise vegetables; keep cow and poultry; house stands on high terraced ground; gas and modern improvements; excellent table; pleasant surroundings; a very desirable summer home. References and further particulars on application.

CHARLES HIGHAM—Hotel. Five minutes' walk; accommodate 50; adults $10, children $5, transient $2; discount to season guests.

Benton Carpenter—Point Pleasant Farm. 3 miles; free transportation; accommodate 30; adults $6; special season rates for families; fine view of Shawangunk Mountains; large shaded lawn; healthful home; raise own vegetables; abundance of fresh milk, eggs and poultry. City references and circulars.

J. Shafer—Private boarding-house. Near depot; accommodate 4; adults $5; house is situated in the suburbs of the city; high ground; splendid views; healthy air for invalids; good table; pleasant walks and drives; excellent water. References on application. Address 62 Grand Avenue, Middletown, N. Y.

John T. Ogden—5 Mulberry Street. Accommodate 4; adults $7.

S. M. Nash—Madison House. ½ mile; accommodate 100; adults $5 to $7, children half, transient $2; discount to season guests.

S. Gausmann—Accommodate 8; adults $6. Full particulars on application.

Mrs. A. P. Carr—Farm-house. 4 miles; accommodate 15; adults $5, children $3.

N. E. Conkling—The Willows Hotel. 1 mile; accommodate 25; adults $10, children $5, transient $2.

Frank A. Moffit—Boarding-house. 2 miles; accommodate 20; adults $4.50, children $3.50, transient $1.

E. A. Brown & Son—Russell House. ¼ mile; accommodate 75; adults $10.50 to $14, children the same, transient $2 to $3.

H. M. Davis—Farm-house. Accommodate 10; adults $6, children $3.

Charles Newkirk—Farm-house. 2½ miles; accommodate 8; adults $6, children $5, transient $1.

MIDDLETOWN STATION—Pine Bush Post-Office.

Mrs. R. L. Thompson—Home comforts; pleasure and good board found at Veerkeerderkill House; no Jews need apply; adults preferred. Rates, references and full particulars upon application.

S. E. Hallet—Ulsterville House. 2 miles. Terms and full particulars on application.

C. A. Jordan—Grand View House. Accommodate 20. Terms and particulars on application.

Mrs. Sarah Vernooy—Village residence. Adults $5. Full particulars on application.

A. B. Jordan (Circleville Post-Office)—Boarding-house. Accommodate 30. Rates and particulars on application.

H. S. Wilkison (Circleville Post-Office)—Accommodate 20; adults $5 to $7. Write for particulars.

Britton Polley (Circleville Post-Office)—Accommodate 10; adults $6. Write for particulars.

Harlan P. Hall (Ridgebury Post-Office)—Accommodate 30; adults $6, children $3. Particulars on application.

Mrs. H. E. Jansen (Crawford Post-Office)—Farm-house. Adults $7. Write for full particulars.

WINTERTON, Sullivan Co.

This is a small village in the town of Mamakating, about 600 feet above the sea. The foot-hills of the Shawangunk Mountains commence just west of the village. To the right and left, extending far into the dim distance, the mighty front of the Shawangunk appears like an unbroken, advancing billow. Our way leads to the right, along the eastern slope, gradually climbing the range.

66 MILES FROM NEW YORK.
FARE, $1.02;
EXCURSION, $2.00.

WINTERTON STATION—Winterton Post-Office.

J. C. LOCKWOOD—Farm-house. ¼ mile; 5 large and airy rooms; adults $6, children $3 to $4; discount to season guests; free transportation; picturesque scenery; high and healthy location; situated on the east side of Shawangunk Mountains; plenty of shade; abundance of fruit; comfortable beds; excellent water; raise own vegetables; croquet and piano; no pains spared for the comfort of guests. References on application.

H. S. COLLARD—Summer home for boarders, with good board, and a desire to meet the wants of those seeking health and rest; very large and airy rooms; healthy location; picturesque scenery; ¼ mile from station. Rates and references on application.

W. W. WINTER—Breezy Heights Boarding-house. Close to station; accommodate 20; adults $7, limited number of children taken, transient $1; discount to season guests; beautiful scenery; healthy climate; never without a breeze; rooms large and airy; good gunning and fishing; raise own vegetables; good livery attached; 2 mails daily to and from New York. Refers to Dr. J. F. Chariveau, 31 West 60th Street, New York.

GEORGE NORBURY—Farm-house. 1 mile; accommodate 10; rates on application; free transportation; raise our own vegetables; boating free; pleasant situation; very healthy; pure water; comfortable rooms; good table. References on application.

GEORGE T. MARSH—Farm-house. Accommodate 18; adults $6, children $3.

Shawangunk Mountains.

BLOOMINGBURGH, SULLIVAN CO.

One of the historic towns of Sullivan County, celebrated by Washington Irving in his "Hans Schwartz." In the colonial period it was a frontier town on the western border of civilization, and suffered much from Indian raids and hostilities. It is 757 feet above the sea, and has a magnificent landscape of mountain and forest, lake and stream. For a long time this town of Mamakating, with its two villages of Bloomingburgh and Wurtsboro, was the business centre of an extensive region of country. The hunting and fishing are excellent, several good trout streams and two or three small lakes being found in the vicinity, and the mountain abounds in game. There are good hotels, and thirty or forty private families who will take summer boarders.

88 MILES FROM NEW YORK.
FARE, $1.98;
EXCURSION, $3.00.

BLOOMINGBURGH STATION—Bloomingburgh Post-Office.

CHAS. F. BENNETT—Terwilliger House. 1 mile; accommodate 40; discount to season guests; free transportation; shady verandas on two stories; rooms cool and airy; no malaria; croquet and tennis grounds; boating and bathing near house; good bass and pickerel fishing; raise our own vegetables; first-class livery attached to the house; 5 minutes' walk to church. References on application.

Mrs. E. GAUDINEER—Boarding-house. 1 mile; accommodate 30; adults $7; reduction for families; large house; shady lawns; mountain air; good table; all the comforts of a good country home; pickerel and bass fishing in the Shawangunk Kill adjoining premises; boats for use of guests; raise our own vegetables; pure milk; convenient livery accommodations. For references and full particulars call on or address Chas. Gaudineer, 552 Grand Street, New York; telephone, Spring 393. Jews will please not apply.

Mrs. F. R. DRAKE—Shady Dell Boarding-house. 1 mile; accommodate 25; terms on application; discount to season guests; large house, well ventilated; extensive lawns, well shaded; piazza on three sides of house; good fishing and boating. References on application.

JEREMIAH EVENS—Locust Hill Farm, situated on the east side of Shawangunk Mountains. 5 miles; accommodate 20; adults $5 to $7, children half; free transportation to season guests; house open the year round; raise our own vegetables; good fishing; lake on farm; boating, bathing and good gunning; take guests out riding at reasonable charge; plenty of shade; fruit in season.

P. W. REDFIELD—Farm-house. Terms and references on application; reduction to families and season guests; raise our own vegetables; plenty of shade; abundance of milk, eggs, poultry, etc.; 5 minutes from church and post-office; excellent table; delightful walks and drives.

A. E. BENSEL—Rose Hill Cottage. 3 miles; accommodate 20; adults $6, children reduction, transient $1; free transportation; located near the Shawangunk Mountains; pure water; boating and bathing; fine drives and walks; daily mail; large grounds; ample shade; piano; all outdoor amusements; table well supplied with dairy and farm products. Refers to Mr. and Mrs. E. P. Clark, 425 Fifth Street, Brooklyn, N. Y.

ALONG THE ROAD TO WHITE LAKE.

W. W. OLIVER—Farm-house. 2 miles; accommodate 18; terms on application; free transportation; raise our own vegetables; boats free to guests; first-class table, well supplied with fruit, fresh eggs and milk; good livery attached. References on application.

Mrs. LEWIS BELL—Shady Lawn Farm House. ½ mile; accommodate 20; adults $5 to $7, children half; discount to season guests; raise our own vegetables; good gunning and fishing; ¼ mile from church; healthy and pleasant location; pure, bracing air; charming scenery; near water. Refers to Chief Engineer Geo. W. Stivers, 303 Vanderbilt Avenue, Brooklyn, N. Y.

Mrs. C. W. MANCE—Farm-house. 1 mile; accommodate 10; adults $6 to $7; healthy location; plenty of eggs, milk, poultry; pure water; beautiful shade; airy rooms; good fishing and boating; raise own vegetables. References on application.

F. J. LEWIS—Cosey Nook Farm House. 3 miles; accommodate 10; adults $6, children $3, transient $1.50; free transportation; raise own vegetables; no malaria or mosquitoes; have own livery; good table; near church. References on application.

JAMES HAIRE—Cold Brook Farm. 2½ miles; accommodate 25; adults $6, children reduction; discount to season guests; daily mails; beautiful shade; no Jews wanted; near mountain; raise own vegetables; will try to please guests. References on application.

Mrs. HENRIETTA BAIRD—Farm-house. 3 miles; accommodate 18; adults $6, transient $1; have our own livery; bath in house; piano and organ; will meet guests at station; trout pond on premises; raise own vegetables; excellent table. References on application.

Mrs. DAVID H. SCOTT—Farm-house. 1 mile; accommodate 12; adults $6, children under 10 years $3, transient $1; raise own vegetables; good fishing and gunning; 5 minutes' walk to church; first-class livery; piazza in front of house; plenty of shade; excellent water; convenient to post-office. References on application.

Mrs. A. NORRIS—Maple Grove Farm. 2½ miles; accommodate 30; adults $6, children $3 to $4; free transportation to and from depot; house located on public road; high, dry and healthy; surrounded by fine shady lawn and walks; large rooms; pure water; raise our own vegetables; boating and fishing near by; boats free to guests; well adapted for the enjoyment and comfort of guests. Correspondence solicited.

A. T. McEWEN—Farm-house. 1 mile; accommodate 25; free transportation; very desirable place; cottage in same yard suitable for a large family or party; near village; high location; charming views; mountain air; good water; large piazza; ample shade; spacious lawn; no Hebrews taken; raise our own vegetables; plenty of fresh butter, milk and eggs; near church; keep our own livery; stabling for horses. References on application, and rates.

Mrs. J. C. GOWDEY—Boarding-house. 1 mile; accommodate 30; 16 rooms; adults $7, no children, transient $1.50; discount for season, also for cottage rooms suitable for young men; transportation from depot 15 cents, trunks 25 cents; good fishing in lake and river; boats free; convenient to church; no malaria; ample shade; house on high ground; piano and croquet and tennis lawn, swings and hammocks. References on application. House opens May 1st. Special rates for May and June.

Mrs. ANNIE BENNETT—Farm-house. 4 miles; accommodate 10; adults $5, children $3 to $5, transient $1; 1,800 feet above tide-water; free transportation; plenty of shade; pure spring water; splendid milk; have our own cows and make our own butter; raise our own vegetables; good fishing and gunning; livery on farm; 3 miles to church. Write for full particulars.

WILLIAM H. ELLIS—Mountain View House. Accommodate 35; terms on application; free boats for guests; for attractions of house and surroundings send for circular; good table. Refers to D. F. Fowler, 1239 Bedford Avenue, Brooklyn; G. B. Thorne, 238 Nostrand Avenue, Brooklyn; Thomas Young, 37 Murray Street, New York.

Mrs. SARAH BARRETT—Boarding-house, cottage home. ¾ mile; accommodate 20; adults $6, children half, transient $1; good fishing in Shawangunk Lake—trout, pickerel and bass; first-class livery accommodation; church near by; good table; pure and bracing air; charming surroundings. References and particulars on application.

Mrs. MILO SEAGEARS—Centreview House. Will be opened for summer guests June 1st, 1892; parties accommodated at any season of the year; terms, number accommodated, references and description of place on application. P. O. Box 179.

THE GREAT CREVICE. *(Two miles from Ellenville.)*

Mrs. DAVID D. LOW—Farm-house. 1 mile; accommodate 30; adults $6, children $4, transient $1; discount to season guests; raise our own vegetables; good fishing; boats and fishing-tackle; good livery; near church; large shady yard; large piazzas in front and back of house; free transportation. References on application.

DELL CASE—Shorter House. 1 mile; accommodate 25; adults $7, children half; discount to season guests; good boating, fishing and hunting; pure air; no malaria; good livery; fine drives. Refers to Benj Weeks, 56 Washington Market, New York, and J. W. Haarew, 338 Greenwich Street, New York.

Mrs. J. H. DOSS—Farm-house. ½ mile; accommodate 40; adults $7, children $3.50, transient $1.50; discount to season guests; free transportation; pleasant rooms; beautiful shade; balcony 50 feet long; table abundantly supplied with fresh butter, milk and eggs; excellent gunning and fishing; good livery; near church. References on application.

Mrs. GEORGE BARRETT—Adults $6. Full particulars on application.

EDWARD H. MILLS—Farm-house. Accommodate 25. Terms on application.

WILLIAM ANDREWS—Accommodate 10. Correspondence solicited.

Mrs. BETHUEL DOOLITTLE—Farm-house. 3 miles; accommodate 5; adults $5 to $6.

J. H. HOWARD—Private residence. Accommodate 10. Terms and full particulars on application.

REUBEN COCHRAN—Maple Vale Cottage. 2 miles; accommodate 14; adults $5, children under twelve $4, transient $1.

HIGH VIEW, SULLIVAN CO.

BLOOMINGBURGH STATION—High View Post-Office.

For the convenience of residents and guests of summer boarding-houses situated near the Bloomingburgh depot, the Government recently established a post-office near the station, calling it " High View." This is a great convenience to that locality, and saves a trip of a mile and a half down into the valley to the village of Bloomingburgh for the mail.

The summer boarding-houses about High View Post-Office are situated at an elevation of about 950 feet above the sea on the eastern slope of the Shawangunk Mountains, and command from their lofty situation broad and extensive views, embracing several hundred square miles of mountain, forest, lake and stream.

High View has many attractions for those seeking a cool, dry and invigorating atmosphere, with excellent boating, gunning and fishing among the numerous trout streams and small lakes in its vicinity.

Near Bloomingburgh Station the railway enters a tunnel, 3,800 feet in length, which penetrates the Shawangunk Mountains 750 feet above tide-water and about 520 feet below its summit. The tunnel passed, the railway descends toward the Mamakating Valley.

BLOOMINGBURGH STATION—High View Post-Office.

D. G. CARPENTER—Overlook Place, private boarding-house. ¼ mile from railroad station, post-office and telegraph; accommodate 50; adults $7 to $9, transient $1.50 per day; limited number of children; no Hebrews; situated high up on Shawangunk mountain side; magnificent view; piazza 90 feet long, overlooking 1,000 square miles; tennis, croquet, piano; pure drinking-water; good drainage; liberal table; pure milk as free as water; transient accommodations for parties prospecting for summer board; carriage meets any train free of charge, if notified by letter or telegram; reasonable livery rates for visiting the numerous boarding-houses in the vicinity. Circulars on application.

OVERLOOK PLACE—D. G. CARPENTER.

ISAAC P. BENNETT—High View House. Accommodate 100 (built in 1889 and enlarged for 1892); opens June 1st; adults $7 to $12, transient $1.50; no Hebrews; only five minutes to station and post-office; situated on "Breezy Summit" (an eastern off-set of Shawangunk Mountains); 250 feet above the village and plains below, about 1,000 feet above the sea, overlooking a grand panorama of over 1,000 square miles of mountain forest, lake and stream, framed in by Fishkill, Skunemunk, Storm-King, and Crow's Nest Mountains at Cornwall, which, although 30 miles away, are plainly visible, also "Sam's Point"; 30 acres land; spacious lawns surrounding house, with nice grove and glen; tennis, croquet, hammocks, swings, organ and piano; perfect drainage; liberal table, supplied with own productions; transient and livery accommodation for prospectors for summer board will be instantly and reasonably furnished by calling at my store and post-office, near the station. Circulars on application.

Mrs. E. S. CONKLING—Old-fashioned farm-house. ¼ mile from depot; accommodate 10; no style; adults $6, children under 12 half price; boarders at all seasons, and unattended children a specialty. Correspondence solicited.

WILLIAM L REDFIELD—Farm-house. ¼ mile; accommodate 12; rates and references on application; free transportation; cool rooms; excellent board; milk, eggs, poultry; good water and ample shade; music, croquet; four daily meals.

Mrs. LEWIS BURNS—Boarding-house. ½ mile; accommodate 15; adults $6; situated on high ground; pure mountain air; pleasant surroundings, commanding extensive views; good water; large rooms; plenty of fresh vegetables. References and full particulars on application.

Mrs. A. W. Miller—Farm-house. ¼ mile; accommodate 25 to 30; adults $6 to $7, transient $1.25; free transportation; raise own vegetables; location perfectly healthful; pleasantly situated on the eastern slope of the Shawangunk Mountains. References: Joseph F. Gray, M.D., 326 W. 31st Street, New York; C. A. Decker, 46 Wall Street, New York.

J. G. Blake—Farm-house. ¼ mile; accommodate 30; adults $6, children under 10 years half rate; elevated location; free transportation; good livery convenient; 1 mile from church; raise own vegetables; plenty of good milk. References on application.

Virgil Godfrey—Farm-house. 5 minutes' walk; accommodate 20; terms on application; situated on eastern slope of the Shawangunk; 1 mile from church; plenty of fresh eggs, butter and milk; ample shade; raise own vegetables. Write for further particulars.

Joseph McConbray—High View Hotel. Near station; accommodate 20; terms reasonable; house newly furnished; good livery attached; pleasant location; excellent table; large and airy rooms. References on application.

N. B. Horton—Hillside Farm. 1 mile; accommodate 30; adults $7, children $3.50; free transportation; raise our own vegetables; splendid location; fine drives; good livery. Correspondence solicited; terms and references on application.

BLOOMINGBURGH STATION—Burlingham Post-Office.

B. E. Godfrey—Farm-house. 5 miles; accommodate 17; adults $7, children under 7 years $3.50, over 7 years $4, transient $1; free transportation; have a large and good garden; good fishing in Shawangunk creek; guests taken to church free of charge; telephone to connect with telegraph office; livery on farm; rooms are large, with high ceilings, and well ventilated; good beds and excellent water; first-class table; fresh eggs and ice-cold milk; daily mail; large shady lawn; 32 feet of piazza. Write for particulars.

Mrs. J. Coddington—Accommodate 10. Terms and full particulars on application.

Sarah J. Bennett—Farm-house. Accommodate 12; adults $5, children half rates.

BLOOMINGBURGH STATION—Walker Valley Post-Office.

R. W. Morrow—Hotel. 5 miles; accommodate 20; adults $5 to $6, children $3 to $4, transient $1; free transportation; pleasant surroundings; raise our own vegetables; large and airy rooms; healthy location; plenty of fresh milk; good trout-fishing; good gunning; first-class livery; romantic walks and drives; excellent table; pure and bracing air; excellent water. References on application.

George U. Evans—Mount Pleasant House. 6 miles; accommodate 40; 21 rooms; adults $5 to $6, children $3, transient $1; free transportation; good fishing and gunning; horses and carriages can be obtained by guests at reasonable rates; plenty of fresh milk, eggs and butter; rooms large and well ventilated; raise our own vegetables; good table; berries of all kinds and chickens; no Jews taken; grand view of the Shawangunk Mountains and Wallkill Valley; nice shaded lawn; charming glen, with a stream of water flowing through it, within walking distance; very romantic and attractive spot. Elevation 2,000 feet. References on application.

S J. Miller—Brookside Farm. 5 miles; accommodate 20; 11 rooms; adults $5 to $6, children $3 to $4, transient $1; discount to season guests; free transportation; high ground, overlooking large portion of Orange and Ulster counties; 6 miles from Sam's Point, with an elevation of 2,422 feet; raise our own vegetables; the best of water; 1 mile from church; keep team for the accommodation of guests; plenty of nuts and fruit in season; very healthful. Refers to Chas. S. Fowler, 455 Willoughby Avenue, Brooklyn, or 9 Elizabeth Street, New York, and H. Freeman, 814 Grand Street, Jersey City, N. J.

WURTSBORO, Sullivan Co.

90 MILES FROM NEW YORK.
FARE, $2.04;
EXCURSION, $3.47.

As the train emerges from the tunnel, and rounds the curve beyond, a splendid view of the village of Wurtsboro, in the Mamakating Valley, greets the eye. Its well-kept, shady, level streets and the mountainous sur-

VEERKEERDERKILL FALLS. (97 *feet high, near Sam's point.*)

roundings attract all who see it. It was incorporated in 1866, and has a population of about 500; there are several good hotels, and numerous boarding-houses in and about the village. Its three churches—Catholic, Dutch Reformed, and Methodist—are as fine edifices as can be found in a country village. Well connected by telephone, postal, and W. U. Telegraph; two New York mails daily; a good livery stable; fine drives and picnic groves; well-stocked trout streams in and near by; good hunting in season within six miles (Wurtsboro being the nearest station), is the great fishing-ground of Sullivan County, comprising five lakes, viz., Yankee, Wolf, McKee, Foulwood, and Masten.

The absence of factories insures to the weary citizen of the metropolis complete rest, pure and bracing air, while the water is the very best. Among those who will accommodate city guests this season are the following:

WURTSBORO STATION—Wurtsboro Post-Office.

FRANK McCUNR—Dorrance House. 1 mile; accommodate 50; discount to season guests; free transportation; house centrally located; rooms cool and airy; abundance of shade; table furnished with the best in the market; good fishing, hunting and boating; boats free to guests; telephone and telegraph; two New York mails daily; livery attached to the house; fine drives; accommodations for those wishing to bring their own horses and carriages. Parties visiting Wurtsboro and vicinity, looking for board, will find good accommodations at the Dorrance House, and livery will be furnished with competent and well-informed drivers to convey parties around the country; charges reasonable. References on application.

EDITH VAN KURAN—Private residence. 10 minutes' walk from depot; accommodate 16; adults $6; a desirable summer home; large, airy rooms newly furnished; excellent table; pure milk; raise our own vegetables; picturesque scenery; romantic walks and drives; healthy location. Refers to Dr. E. F. Quinlian, 308 W. 20th Street, New York.

J. W. PARSELLS—"The Glen," boarding-house. 1 mile; accommodate 20; adults $6, children $3, transient $1; ten large, airy rooms; three churches within 10 minutes' walk; shady walks and romantic surroundings; raise our own vegetables; trout stream running through grounds; hammock and swings. References on application.

Mrs. ELMER SMITH—Private house. 1 mile; accommodate 10; adults $6, children over 10 years $4; pleasant surroundings; good table. Further information cheerfully given on application. Refers to A. B. Wilson, 755 Seventh Ave., New York; T. B. Morrison, 693 E. 143d Street, New York.

KATE C. MUNN—Hotel and farm-house. 3 miles; accommodate 25; rates on application; transient $1.50; good trout, bass and pickerel fishing in Masten, Wolf, and Yankee ponds; 2 miles from church; pleasant walks and drives; good table. References and full particulars on application.

HENRY GRAHAM—Farm-house. 2 miles; accommodate 10; adults $6, children $3; discount for season guests; good fishing; raise own vegetables; good gunning, near Bashaw creek; excellent table; picturesque scenery. References and full particulars on application.

G. H. OLCOTT—Olcott House. ½ mile; accommodate 60; adults $6 to $7, transient $1; discount to season guests; raise our own vegetables; romantic walks and drives; free from malaria and hay-fever; excellent trout, bass and pickerel fishing; good partridge, quail, woodcock and duck shooting; three churches near; good table. References and particulars on application.

Mrs. FRED HARDING—Seaside Place. Accommodate 10; adults $5 to $6.

Mrs. WALTER FUCHS—Watercress Farm. Accommodate 10; terms $5 to $6.

T. V. MASTEN—Accommodate 10. Full particulars on application.

HENRY W. BUDD—Mountain View Boarding-house. 4 miles; accommodate 35; adults $6 to $10, transient $1.25; raise our own vegetables; good fishing in Masten, Yankee, Wolf and Fowlwood lakes; boats free; very best of gunning—partridge, woodcock and rabbit; livery accommodation; about 1,400 feet above sea-level; fine trout streams near by; location particularly adapted for those afflicted with throat and lung troubles. References and all other particulars on application.

WILLIAM T. HARDING—Hotel and boarding-house. Accommodate 50; adults $5 to $8, children half rates.

CHARLES REILLEY—Commercial Hotel. Accommodate 50; adults $6 to $7.

WURTSBORO STATION—Rock Hill Post-Office.

Mrs. JOHN LORD—Farm-house. 6 miles; accommodate 20; adults $6 to $7; transportation in private conveyance 50 cents; two lakes within 10 minutes' walk from house; good fishing and gunning; boats free to guests; trout stream on farm; elevation 1,200 feet; bracing air. References on application.

BENJAMIN LORD—Farm-house. 6 miles; accommodate 30; adults $6, children $3; six lakes within 2 miles of house; excellent fishing—all kinds of fish; boats free to guests on Lord and McKee lakes. References on application.

SANFORD BURTIS—Six Lake House. 5 miles; accommodate 25; adults $5, children reduction; trout brooks near by; six lakes within one mile and a half from the house, well stocked with bass and pickerel; daily mail. References and full particulars on application.

GEO. D. ROYCE—Farm-house. 8 miles; terms on application; near three lakes; one mile from the river; romantic surroundings; raise own vegetables; good table; pure water; bracing air. References and full particulars will be cheerfully given.

MARGARETTA MCKEE—Lakeside Grove House. 6½ miles of mountain ride; accommodate 11; adults $6 to $7; elevation 1,500 feet; grand and extensive views; constant breeze; McKee Lake in front of house; numerous lakes within 10 minutes' walk; excellent bass and pickerel fishing; good gunning; fine grove near house. Full particulars and references on application.

FRANKLIN JOHNSON—Farm-house. 7 miles; accommodate 8. Terms on application.

SUMMITVILLE, SULLIVAN CO.

The junction point with the branch line to Ellenville. Within a short distance of the station are located several very desirable farm and boarding houses, situated high up on the mountain overlooking the entire length of the Mamakating Valley.

94 MILES FROM NEW YORK. FARE, $2.13; EXCURSION, $3.60.

SUMMITVILLE STATION—Summitville Post-Office.

CHARLES CUDNEY—Mount Vernon Farm House. 2 miles; accommodate 40; 20 rooms; adults $4 to $6, children $2.50 to $4, transient $1; discount to season guests; free transportation; this house is situated on the Delaware Mountains, 1,200 feet above the sea-level; pure spring water; plenty of shade; fruit and berries in abundance; raise our own vegetables; excellent trout-fishing in Masten Pond; good livery at house; gunning—partridge and woodcock; ¼ mile to church. References on application.

JOHN I. CUDNEY—Mount Vernon Farm House. 3½ miles; accommodate 25; adults $4 to $6, children reduction, transient $1.25; free transportation; house situated at an elevation of 1,200 feet on range of Delaware Mountains; 63 feet of piazza; pleasant walks; pure spring water; plenty of shade; trout brook running through farm; plenty of milk and eggs; raise our own vegetables; good gunning; good livery; near church. References on application.

Port Jervis, Monticello & New York R.R.

At Summitville connection is made in Union Station with the trains of this road. Leaving Summitville, the line follows the beautiful Mamakating Valley to Huguenot Junction, and from there traverses the picturesque Neversink Valley and the wild country adjacent to Monticello. During the season of summer travel, through day coaches and drawing-room cars will run from Weehawken to Monticello. This will obviate any changing of cars at Summitville, and passengers boarding the cars at Weekawken will go through without change to destination. Through tickets are issued and baggage checked to destination.

HUGUENOT, Orange Co.

Celebrated for its good hotel and the famous Huguenot Chalybeate Springs, which are being extensively introduced and used as a remedy for those afflicted with rheumatism, dyspepsia, scrofula, liver and kidney complaints, diseases peculiar to females, and as a general purifier of the blood. Though but recently discovered, the virtues of the waters have been attested by many with beneficial and remarkable results in the cure of diseases.

| 112 MILES FROM NEW YORK. |
| LIMITED FARE, $2.33; |
| EXCURSION, $3.60. |

CUDDEBACKVILLE STATION—Cuddebackville Post-Office.

LEVI CUDDEBACK—Hotel Caudebec, hotel and boarding-house. Five minutes' walk from depot; 25 rooms; accommodate 50; adults $7 to $10, transient $1.50 to $2; nothing intoxicating sold; hotel is enlarged and newly furnished; situated on high ground; building is three stories high, with a mansard roof and broad piazzas in front; fine roads and mountain paths leading out from the hotel; in the midst of trout streams; excellent fishing in the Neversink and Bashaskill; good gunning—partridge, woodcock and rabbit; near church; raise our own vegetables. References exchanged.

The Ellenville Branch.

THE ELLENVILLE BRANCH, which is eight miles long, is of considerable importance. The first station on this branch is

PHILLIPSPORT, SULLIVAN CO.

A pleasant little village on the Delaware & Hudson Canal. Two churches and a good hotel. There are several private families in the vicinity who are willing to receive summer boarders. The prices are reasonable and the accommodations good.

95 MILES FROM NEW YORK. FARE, $2.19; EXCURSION, $3.77.

PHILLIPSPORT STATION—Phillipsport Post-Office.

ISAAC BUDD—Farm-house. 1 mile; accommodate 30; terms on application; transient $1; discount to season guests; good fishing; lake one hundred yards from house; boats free to guests; raise own vegetables; good livery; ½ mile to church; house on high ground; good spring and well water; large yard and plenty of shade; safe place for children; plenty of play-ground; house in full view of lake; free transportation. References: Ralph Henry, 575 Leonard Street, Brooklyn, N. Y.; Dr. D. F. King, 651 Lexington Avenue, Brooklyn, N. Y.; F. A. Wall, 137 W. 127th Street, New York.

Mrs. CARRIE A. ALLEN—Farm-house. 1 mile; accommodate 12; rates low; free transportation; excellent trout-fishing in Trout Fall Brook; romantic walks and drives; commands a fine view of the surrounding country; good gunning; excellent table; 1 mile from church; raise own vegetables; discount to season guests. Full particulars and references on application.

ELIJAH BUDD—Farm-house. ¼ mile from station; accommodate 20; adults $5, children reduction, transient $1; free transportation; gunning; raise our own vegetables; 1 mile west of Shawangunk Mountains; high ground; large yard around house; plenty of shade; ½ mile from church. Refers to J. B. Dodd, 270 Broadway, New York; F. J. Bull, Assistant Superintendent Madison Square Garden, 256 W. 43d Street, New York.

CORNELIUS TICE—Adults $6, children $3. Write for particulars.

SPRING GLEN, SULLIVAN CO.

FARE, $2.25. EXCURSION, $3.89.

A quiet peaceful village, surrounded by delightful scenery.

SPRING GLEN STATION—Spring Glen Post-Office.

J. B. HAWXHURST & P. TICE—Farm-house. 1 mile; accommodate 20; adults $6 to $7, children reduction, transient $1; free transportation; pleasantly situated, overlooking the village; attractive and healthy; nice shady lawn; liberal table. Refer to William T. Blessing, 24 New York Avenue, Brooklyn, N. Y.; I. Dusel, 11 Warren Street, New York.

ELLENVILLE FROM THE EAST.

SANFORD CUDNEY—Farm-house. ½ mile; accommodate 20; adults $6, children reduction; free transportation; splendid view of Shawangunk Mountains; plenty of shade; good water; pleasant walk to Buttermilk Falls; nice drive to Sam's Point, Ice-Caves, Honk Fal's and other places of interest.

SANFORD I. TICE—Farm-house. 1½ miles; accommodate 20; adults $7 to $8, transient $2 to $u.50.

JOHN H. THORNTON—Boarding-house. Accommodate 12; near station; adults $6, children $3, transient $1.

ELLENVILLE, ULSTER CO.

Terminus of the Ellenville Branch. Three and a half hours from New York. Through passenger service during the summer season. A charming village of about 3,500 inhabitants, situated in the heart of the Shawangunk region, 340 feet above the sea. It has many delightful drives, and from near-by points are to be gained the most magnificent views of natural scenery to be found in the East. Within a few miles of Mohonk, Minnewaska, Meenahga and other celebrated resorts. Many of the noted trout streams of Ulster and Sullivan and the fishing lakes of the latter county are within easy driving distance. Among the bits of natural scenery of the immediate vicinity are Sam's Point, a rocky ledge crowning the highest of the Shawangunk summits; the Ice-Caves—natural openings in the mountain—where ice and snow are found the year round, and Minnewaska, Honk, Hanging Rock and other beautiful cascades and waterfalls. The village of Ellenville has well-paved and shaded streets, and is lighted with gas. Many of the hotels and boarding-houses of the region are connected by telephone with one another and with the Hudson river system. There are many fine residences, six churches, excellent schools, and the place is noted for the intelligence, refinement and sobriety of its people and the healthfulness of its climate.

101 MILES FROM NEW YORK. FARE $2.37; EXCURSION. $4.13.

ELLENVILLE STATION—Ellenville Post-Office.

WILLIAM H. WESER—Boarding-house. Accommodate 100; terms $7 to $10, transient $2; special terms to season guests; large, light, airy rooms, neatly furnished; running water on every floor; good table; vegetables and fruit from farm of 150 acres; church ½ mile; livery accommodations; daily mails; advantageously situated on the western range of Catskill Mountains, 1,800 feet above sea-level; one hour's drive, replete with beautiful scenery, from Ellenville Station, over a well-graded road; large pine grove five minutes' walk from house; fine views of Lakes Mohonk and Minnewaska—also Roundtop and High Peak; Hanging Rock Falls three miles distant. References: Henry Vogt, 105 Kent Ave., Brooklyn; James J. Curtin, with Brokaw Brothers, Fourth Avenue and Astor Place, New York; H. C. Dodge, 406 West Fifty-first Street, New York; Dr. Lawrence, Bedford Avenue and North Sixth Street, Brooklyn; Dr. R. Catle, 457 West Thirty-fourth Street, New York; R. I. Bush, 872 Sixth Avenue, New York.

ROBERT J. GEILHARD—Boarding-house. 5 miles; accommodate 50; 27 sleeping-rooms; rates on application; transient $1.50; raise everything; first-class livery; comfortable conveyance from house 75 cents per head, trunks 25 and 50 cents; ½ mile from church; situated on Shawangunk Mountains; elevation 2,100 feet; piazza 126 feet in length, from which can be viewed a panorama in grandeur and compass unsurpassed in any other section of the Eastern States. Sam's Point thirty minutes' walk from house; Bear Hill (Southern Cliff) only five minutes' walk from house; considered the finest point for views on the Shawangunk range; grand ascents for the venturesome; quiet, shady, cool walks for those desiring quiet and rest; ice-cold running water on every floor; milk, vegetables, etc., from own farm; livery at moderate rates: terms on application, stating requirements. Send for circular.

F. J. FARR—Mount Mongola Boarding-house. 3 miles; accommodate 60; terms $7 to $12; discount to season guests; situated on the Shawangunk Mountains; house is located at an elevation of 2,000 feet above tide-water, commanding a fine view of the surrounding country; it is a large four-story structure, containing large rooms neatly furnished and well ventilated; large dining-room and parlor, with cheerful open fireplaces; 170 feet of broad piazza, surrounded by fine shade trees and lawn. City visitors will find this part of the Shawangunk Mountains particularly interesting and enjoyable; daily mail; Sam's Point, Ice-Caves, Honk Falls and other places of interest near by. Send for circular. Refers to John A. Davis, 336 West Forty-eighth Street, New York; W. H. Hollywell, 28 Watts Street, New York; Mrs. T. Christie, 247 Seventh Street, Brooklyn, N. Y.; P. Higgins, 15 Pearl Street, Brooklyn, N. Y.; Mrs. C. E. Stevens, 107 South Elliott Street, Brooklyn, N. Y.

STEPHEN ERNHOUT—Summer residence, "Breeze Lawn." 2 miles; accommodate 25; terms $7 to $15, children under eight years $5, transient $1.25; charge for transportation 40 cents; good fishing; all kinds of game; good livery accommodations; saddle horses and a newly built barn; have 17 acres surrounding the house, in which are set out in groups some fine evergreen trees; summer houses; good place for lawn tennis and croquet; large green lawn; plenty of flowers, etc. References exchanged.

A. B. GRIMLEY—Maplewood Boarding-house. ¼ mile; accommodate 50; 28 rooms; adults $8 to $12, transient $2; commanding fine view of mountain and valley scenery; grounds border on the Beerkill, laid out with walks, arbors, shade trees, etc.; many objects of interest in the vicinity—Sam's Point, Ice-Caves, besides numerous lakes and waterfalls; fishing and gunning; horses and carriages for use of guests at moderate rates; good stable for guests desiring to bring their own horses. Refers to Dr. H. A. Moore, Elizabeth, N. J.; Francis McArdle, 232 Ross Street, Brooklyn, N. Y.; E. F. Haight, 220 Hooper Street, Brooklyn, N. Y.; Mrs. F. E. Hooker, Orange City, Fla.

LEGRAND W. BOTSFORD—Sam's Point House. Situated at the highest peak of the Shawangunk Mountains, commanding unsurpassing views of unsurpassing beauty and extent; a favorite place of resort for health and enjoyment, where visitors regale in the pure water of the Mary Tanza Lake, and inhale the pure air from the rock-bound caverns lined with ice and snow. Parties wishing board will address LeGrand W. Botsford, Ellenville, N. Y.

Mrs. C. M. NEWKIRK—Hillside Cottage. ½ mile; accommodate 6 to 8; adults $7 to $10, children under fourteen $4 to $6, transient $1; discount to season guests; good gunning and fishing—trout, pickerel, bass, etc.; good livery; 10 minutes' walk to church; pure water, beautiful walks and drives; plenty of shade; splendid scenery and waterfalls. References: Miss A. McCreary, 161 Ross Street, Brooklyn; J. Barker, 117 Hooper Street, Brooklyn, N. Y.

CHARLES H. GEILHARD—"The Wawbeek" Cliff Farm. 4 miles; accommodate 100; terms on application; elevation 2,300 feet; views cannot be surpassed; house, etc., entirely new, and every room commanding a grand view; with balconies and open fireplaces; enlarged 10-foot piazzas running entire length, and covered carriage-way, house, etc.; fitted up especially for comfort of summer boarders. References in circular; send for same and photograph.

Mrs. GEO. IRVIN—Boarding-house. ¼ mile; accommodate 12; adults $7 to $8, children under ten half, transient $1.25; discount to season guests; beautiful mountain scenery; fine drives and walks; excellent livery; raise our own fruit and vegetables; five minutes' walk from church. Refers to John Graham, office New York & Brooklyn Ferry Co., foot of Broadway, Brooklyn, E. D.; Miss A. F. Simpson, 115 Manhattan Street, New York, and Edw. C. Atwood, 1649 Second Avenue, New York.

JOHN KINDBERG—Grove Farm. 5 miles; accommodate 40; adults $7 to $10, transient $1.50; transportation from depot $1; trunks 50 cents; on the summit of Shawangunk Mountains, 1 mile from Sam's Point, at an elevation of 2,200 feet; commands a fine view of Orange and Sullivan counties; liberal table; raise our own vegetables. Full information on application. Open June 15th.

Mrs. E. C. ROBISON—Farm-house. 1½ miles; accommodate 13; adults $6, children $3, transient $1; transportation free; healthy location; plenty of milk, eggs and fruit; good livery accommodation; liberal table; raise our own vegetables. References and full particulars on application.

C. H. LOSIE—Farm-house. 4 miles; accommodate 8; rates on application; discount to season guests; pleasant, well-furnished rooms to let, with or without board; picturesque mountain scenery and landscape views; good gunning and fishing; five minutes' walk to church; good table; romantic walks and drives. Further information on application.

Mrs. W. H. CARMAN—Private boarding-house. ¾ mile; accommodate 12; adults $5 to $7, children $3 to $5, transient $1.25; location quiet, clean and healthy; good water; within two hours' ride of Lake Minnewaska, Sam's Point and Mt. Meenahga; convenient to numerous points of local attraction; good table; good fishing and gunning. Refers to John McElhone, J. B. Keeler, P. M., Ellenville, N. Y.

Mrs. J. M. LOW—Accommodate 20; terms $6 to $9; first-class board; neat, comfortable home; mountain resort; fine views; shady grounds; plenty of milk, cream and farm produce. Write for further particulars.

C. A. VAN WAGENER—Boarding-cottage. ½ mile; accommodate 10; adults $6 to $10; good fishing; trout, bass and pickerel streams; good livery; ½ mile from church; extensive and fine views; large groves, mountain walks, Ice-Caves near; near village with stores, liveries, etc., easy of access. References on application.

ALEX. R. McDOWELL—Boarding and farm house. 3½ miles; accommodate 40; adults $6, children under twelve $3; raise own vegetables; 1½ miles to church; pure mountain air; beautiful scenery and running spring water; table supplied with products of the farm; free transportation. References on application.

JAMES A. MYERS—Terrace Hill House. ¾ mile; accommodate 50; well-ventilated and nicely furnished rooms; terms $7 to $10 per week, transient $1.50; situated on summit of hill, ¼ mile south of village, surrounded by pleasant grounds; table supplied with fruits and vegetables from farm; every comfort for spring and fall guests; horses and carriages, with careful driver, for use of guests, at reasonable rates; accommodation for boarding horses. Please write for circular showing cut of house.

THOMAS PARKER, JR.—Farm-house. 3 miles; accommodate 30; adults $6; discount to season guests; free transportation; house has been enlarged and newly furnished; high, spacious and airy rooms; good table; plenty of milk, eggs and vegetables; daily mail. References on application.

Mrs. GEO. E. EVANS—The Buena Vista Boarding-house. 3 minutes' walk; adults $6 to $7; discount to season guests; rooms large, cool and well furnished; parlors with open fireplaces; house commands a fine view of mountain and valley scenery; grounds handsomely laid out with walks; shade trees, hedges, etc.; many objects of interest in the vicinity—Sam's Point, the highest point in the mountain range, Ice-Caves and many beautiful waterfalls within walking distance; excellent fishing, boating and gunning; horses and carriages for use of guests at moderate rates; 5 minutes from church and post-office; health, rest and recreation await you here. Refers to Miss Weslendorf, 165 E. 66th St., New York; Wm. R. Leach, 131 Fulton St., New York.

ABRAM CONSTABLE—Hotel. ¼ mile; accommodate 30; adults $7 to $12; free transportation; good fishing and gunning; first-class livery; six churches within two blocks. Write for particulars.

U. E. TERWILLIGER—Mount Meenahga Boarding-house and Cottages. 2 miles; accommodate 175; terms $12 to $25, transient $2.50 to $3; transportation from station in stage and private conveyance 75 cents, trunks 25 cents and 50 cents; horses and carriages to let; in connection with this house are seven cottages; a cheery, quiet summer home. Full description of house will be found in reading matter on page elsewhere. References exchanged.

JACOB M. DEWITT—Franklin Farm House. ½ mile; accommodate 12; adults $7 to $10, children under twelve $3, transient $1.50; discount to season guests; free transportation; situated on high ground, commanding a panoramic view of surrounding country; plenty of shade; excellent fishing in trout streams near by. References on application.

JOHN H. DIVINE—To rent, a nice cottage; 8 rooms, well furnished; good organ. Apply to John H. Divine, Ellenville, N. Y.

Mrs. E. KLYNE—Private house. Near depot; accommodate 6 to 8 ladies. Correspondence solicited.

JOHN HABEL—Accommodate 8; adults $5. Correspondence solicited.

GEORGE BLEAKLEY—Farm-house. 4 miles; accommodate 14; adults $8 to $12, children $8, transient $1 50.

MT. MEENAHGA HOTEL

Is located in the Shawangunk Mountains in Ulster County, about two miles from the village and railroad station of Ellenville, at which point stage—a private conveyance—will meet guests, on arrival of any train, upon notification.

Mt. Meenahga was opened in 1883 with accommodations for about forty guests. In 1886 the house was enlarged so as to provide (with the cottages) for one hundred. This season additions have been made making its present capacity 175.

All the buildings are located on a picturesque bluff facing northwest, 1,500 feet above tide-water, and special effort has been made to make them attractive and in harmony with the beautiful natural surroundings.

In connection with the house there are six cottages, from 300 to 1,000 feet distant. These have been built with a view of renting to families desiring the quiet and privacy which a cottage especially affords. Each of them has a sitting-room with open fireplace; from three to five sleeping-rooms, furnished plain but complete with necessary furniture.

From the porch and rooms of each story of the boarding-house and every cottage are enjoyed remarkable mountain and valley views, beautiful not only in their extent and variety, but as well in the clearness and distinctness with which forms and places may be traced. All the prominent peaks of the Catskills, with the smaller mountains intervening; Ellenville and other villages; lakes and winding streams among the hills and along the valleys are all plainly seen with the naked eye, and combine to form a panorama, as seen from this point, equaled by but few of the famous summer resorts. The property comprises 250 acres of wild mountain land, embracing fifty acres under cultivation. From the farm and farms adjoining is furnished an abundance of vegetables, also a full supply of Alderney milk and cream.

MT. MEENAHGA HOTEL.

The season opens June 1st and closes October 1st to 15th. Communications in regard to board, rooms, etc., should be addressed to the proprietor, U. E. Terwilliger, Ellenville, Ulster Co., N. Y.

GREENFIELD, ULSTER CO.

Greenfield, with an elevation of 1,100 feet, is situated four miles from Mountain Dale Station on the main line, and five miles from Ellenville, the terminus of the branch to that place. The drive from Ellenville to Greenfield is along the Beerkill stream, affording one of the most attractive drives in the country. From Mountain Dale the road leads over the hills and affords a magnificent view of the Shawangunk, Catskill and other mountain ranges. Greenfield is well named, as its hills and valleys are always green and bright in the summer season. Its heavy mountain freshets in spring and fall make it one of the cleanest localities in the State. It is well drained by the Beerkill, into which a number of fine trout streams empty. Its public and private lakes and ponds, coupled with its groves, waterfalls and romantic walks, make it one of the most attractive summer resorts in the State, and its accommodations are of a high order. Some 500 boarders fill its houses each season. Has post-office, stores, church and telephone communication with Western Union Telegraph Co. at Ellenville.

ELLENVILLE STATION—Greenfield Post-Office.

WINDSOR LAKE HOTEL.

Is located in the Shawangunk Mountains, Ulster County, five miles from Ellenville, at which station carriages will meet guests on arrival of any train upon notification.

Windsor Lake Hotel was opened in 1885, with accommodations for fifty guests; during the past fall and winter the old building has been taken down, and an entirely new and commodious structure has been erected, so as to provide (with the cottages) for two hundred. The new hotel has all improvements. The halls and stairs are broad; sanitary plumbing throughout; hot and cold water, bath and toilet rooms on every floor; open fireplaces in the parlor, dining-halls, office, and many rooms. Telephone in house, connected with Western Union Telegraph Co.; daily mail.

The main building and cottages are situated on an eminence overlooking the lake, 1,500 feet above tide-water. From the broad piazza, which extends entirely around the hotel, may be had fine views of the surrounding mountain scenery.

A large casino has been erected, containing two fine regulation bowling-alleys on lower floor, with large ball and billiard room on second floor.

Immense lawn for tennis, croquet and archery. The lake is well supplied with good boats, which are free to guests; good fishing hunting, etc.

WINDSOR LAKE HOTEL.

The place abounds in fine views, bluffs and ravines; romantic walks, well shaded. A farm, belonging to Hotel, supplies abundance of vegetables, also a full supply of Alderney milk and cream. The season opens June 1st and closes Oct. 15th. Communications in regard to board, rooms, etc., should be addressed to the proprietor, Paul Nichols, Greenfield, Ulster County, N. Y.

ELLENVILLE STATION—Greenfield Post-Office.

C. L. WINANTS—Quarry Glen Lake House (twelfth season). Accommodate 40: situated on farm of 200 acres, mostly woodland; has private lake with good boats for use of guests ; gravel bottom bathing grounds; romantic walks, fine views, waterfalls, ravines, groves affording fine shade, croquet and lawn tennis grounds, all on the property; house stands on a bluff overlooking the Beaverkill stream; has wide piazza on three sides; good beds; table well supplied; raise our own vegetables; milk from our own dairy. Send for circular.

ADDISON STRATTON—Farm boarding-house on the borders of Sullivan County. 5 miles, accommodate 50; adults $6 to $10, reduction for children ; transportation from depot 50 cents, trunks 25 cents. "The Seven Gables" is situated on high ground; perfect drainage; spring water in house; bath-room; large, airy sleeping-rooms—most of the rooms have two or three large windows; table well supplied with chickens, fresh meats, eggs, milk and cream; daily mail; private telephone; piano, organ, croquet, swings, etc.; abundance of ice; good livery at reasonable rates. Refers to William Hall, 133 E. 69th Street, New York; John H. Bazin, 240 Steuben Street, Brooklyn, N. Y.; J. H. Rimmer, 30 Broad Street, New York; J. M. Newman, care of William Hall's Sons, foot of E. 106th Street, New York. Send for circular.

THE ICE-CAVE. (*Two miles from Ellenville.*)

JOHN H. NEWKIRK—Greenfield Mountain House. 5 miles; accommodate 40; adults $5 to $7; high, pleasant and healthy location; malaria and mosquitoes unknown; pure well and spring water; a large historic grove on farm; 1,400 feet above the sea; a fine cool breeze will be found here in the hottest days. Write for circular.

DAVID PRIDE—Farm-house. 5 miles; accommodate 12; adults $6.

NAPANOCH, ULSTER CO.

This little village is about two miles distant from Ellenville, is very beautiful, and the entire region abounds in "Summer Homes."

ELLENVILLE STATION—Napanoch Post-Office.

GEORGE SCHWAB—Cherry Hill Farm House. 5 miles; accommodate 25; adults $7 to $9, children $3 to $5; good gunning and fishing; first-class table; fresh milk, butter and eggs, and plenty of fruit from premises; pure mountain air; on the banks of a beautiful river and picturesque falls; good accommodations; all large, light rooms; boating, bathing; plenty of shade, etc.; discount to season guests; raise own vegetables. Reference: J. P. Stebbins, 125 W. 47th Street, New York.

H. HUMISTON—Boarding-house. Adults $7 to $10, reduction for children, transient $1.50; discount to season guests; good gunning and fishing; a popular summer resort; pure spring water; bath-room; large, airy sleeping-rooms with good spring-beds; extensive lawn, shaded by large maple-trees; boats free; abundance of milk and cream, chickens, fresh meat and eggs; piano; good livery. Refers to F. Dean, 5th Avenue Bank, New York; H. Henke, 945 Greene Avenue, Brooklyn, N. Y.

GRACE G. DENMAN—Honk Falls Cottage, opens for guests June 15th. Accommodate 10; single rooms $7, two in a room $6; transportation from depot 75 cents; attractive resort for artists and those who want a cool, shady, quiet and healthy place to rest in; raise our own vegetables; fresh milk and eggs, and chickens. References: E. L. Henry, 77 W. 45th Street, New York, and other former guests, on application.

ADOLPH WAGNER—Napanoch House. 2 miles; accommodate 30; rates reasonable; excellent driving, fishing and gunning; boating free; well-shaded lawns; Napanoch Falls, Ice-Caves and Honk Falls are some of the attractions of the place; none but select parties need apply. Refers to E. A. Leitch, and F. Zinke, 72 Broadway, Brooklyn, N. Y.; E. G. Pieper, care of New York Bowery Fire Insurance Co., New York.

ELLENVILLE STATION—Ulster Heights Post-Office.

JOHN BAKER—Sunset View House. 6 miles; accommodate 20; adults $5.50 to $7, children half, transient $1.25; discount to season guests; beautiful scenery; high elevation; pure air; pleasant rooms; raise own vegetables; guests transported to and from the depot free; good fishing and gunning; convenient to church; romantic walks and drives; liberal table; organ in the house; daily mail; fruit and shade trees. References and full particulars on application.

M. F. DILL—Farm-house. 6 miles; accommodate 30; adults $6 to $8, children under ten $3, transient $1.25; free transportation; splendid view of Shawangunk, Catskill, Big Indian, Neversink, Sam's Point Mountains, Ice-Caves, besides numerous waterfalls and lakes; excellent gunning and fishing; good livery; one mile from church; no malaria; good table. References on application.

ELLENVILLE STATION—Mombaccus Post-Office.

ISAAC TRUMBULL—One of the best farm boarding-houses. 10 miles; terms $5 to $6 per week; free transportation to season guests; high, pleasant, healthy locality; good house; liberal table; fifth season; country and mountain scenery unsurpassed; in sight of Lake Mohonk and Minnewaska hotels; fine drives; livery; church and post-office at hand; lake and boats; best of spring water, ice, our own vegetables, milk, butter, etc. For references and particulars, send for circular.

J. H. Low (Montela Post-Office)—Accommodate 25; adults $5, children $3.

The Delaware Mountains.

Returning to the main line at Summitville, we commence at once a rapid ascent of the Delaware Mountains, the high range which, with its outlying spurs, divides the Neversink and Mongaup valleys from the main stream and valley of the Delaware river.

In the eight miles between Summitville and Mountain Dale the ascent is about 420 feet, Mountain Dale being 962 feet above the sea. There are no views in the Catskills or Adirondacks more attractive to the tourist than can be seen from the car windows, as the train winds its serpentine course around the mountain spurs, standing gloomy in their grandeur.

This climbing of the hills continues pretty steadily, though with an occasional stretch of level ground or a slight depression, till Young's Gap, twenty miles further on is reached, where the track of the railway is 1,800 feet above tide-water. The whole region abounds in extensive forests, fine lakes, beetling cliffs of granite, gneiss and older limestones, with some bits so rough and wild that they seem to belong to the ancient realms of chaos; but it has also many beautiful, quiet and charming landscapes, and some so grand as to awaken the admiration and awe of the beholder.

MOUNTAIN DALE, SULLIVAN CO.,

Is a small village, but finely situated on the eastern slope of the Delaware Mountains, 962 feet above the sea. It commands a fine view of the forests, lakes and valleys of the Neversink and Bashaskill. Here are several pleasant homes for summer boarders. The hunting and fishing are excellent.

101 MILES FROM NEW YORK.
FARE, $2.37;
EXCURSION, $4.13.

MOUNTAIN DALE STATION—Mountain Dale Post-Office.

BERNARD LYNCH—Maple Grove Farm House. 1½ miles; accommodate 30; transient $1 ; free transportation to and from depot; raise our own vegetables; good fishing and gunning; first-class livery accommodations; excellent table, plentifully supplied with fresh milk and eggs; shady grounds; daily mail and telegraph; piano; a very pleasant and desirable summer home; charming walks and drives; excellent water; bracing mountain air. References and full particulars on application.

CHARLES DRASSER—Mountain Dale Park House. Ten minutes' walk; accommodate 75; adults $6 to $8, corner rooms $10, rates for children on application, transient $1.50; discount to season guests; excellent trout and pickerel fishing; trout stream on farm; have suitable cottages for parties desiring privacy; raise own vegetables; boats, swings, new large dancing-hall; bowling-alleys, shooting-gallery; splendid gunning; boats free to guests; first-class livery; convenient to church. References on application.

SPRING GROVE HOUSE—A large three-story frame house just built expressly for summer boarders. This house is 600 feet north of, and only about three minutes' walk from, the Mountain Dale Railroad Station and post-office. It will accommodate 50 guests, and will be kept in a first-class manner every way; rates $6 to $10 per week according to room. The house stands on high ground, commanding a view of the entire hamlet and hills round about. The house has all modern conveniences: a large parlor; spacious piazzas and grounds surrounding; 20 good-sized bed-rooms; new furniture throughout; upright piano; window-screens; wood-burning fireplaces in parlor and dining-room. The "Spring Grove House" takes its name from the beautiful five-acre grove immediately in its rear, where are picnic grounds and dancing-pavilions; also perpetual springs of pure water which is supplied by underground pipes to every floor of the house. The drainage of house and grounds has been arranged on a scientific system. Mountain Dale has good express, telegraph and mail facilities. Address, Spring Grove House, Mountain Dale, N. Y.

Mrs. E. G. STODDARD—Linden Lawn House, formerly managed by Elisha Stoddard. ⅛ mile; accommodate 40; adults $6 to $8; reduced rates to season guests; no malaria; living spring water; billiards, bowling-alley, piano; amusement hall 30 by 60; fine recreation and lawn tennis grounds; abundant shade; 65 feet of piazza; boating; church; daily mail and telegraph; raise our own vegetables; swings. References on application.

JOHN T. LYNCH—"Highland Farm" Farm-house. 2 miles; accommodate 75; adults $6 to $8, children reduction, transient $1.50; free transportation to and from train; new house; large and airy rooms, with adjoining rooms for families; elevation 1,400 feet; grand view; pure, living spring water; fine recreation grounds; music; abundance of fruit; raise our own vegetables; table supplied with milk, eggs and butter; double piazza 168 feet long; daily mail; horses and carriages; good hunting and fishing. References on application.

HENRY TERWILLIGER—Farm-house. ½ mile; accommodate 5; adults $5 to 7; guests transported in our own carriage; house surrounded by maple grove and orchard; brook and spring of purest water. References on application.

F. L. MORRIS—Farm-house. ¾ mile; accommodate 30; adults $5 to $6, transient $1; raise our own vegetables; fresh milk, butter and eggs; horses and carriages; near church. References and particulars on application.

JOHN P. COKELET—Farm-house. 1 mile; accommodate 25; adults $5 to $6, children $3, transient $1; discount to season guests; house commands a picturesque view of the surrounding country; cool, large, airy rooms; spacious grounds; mountain air; splendid shade; home-like comforts; pure water; bountiful table; daily mail; telegraph; raise our own vegetables. References and particulars on application.

Mrs. R. MACINTYRE—Prospect Farm House. ½ mile; accommodate 20; adults $6, children according to age; beautifully situated; commanding a fine view of the surrounding country, including Catskill and Shawangunk Mountains; spacious lawn, with croquet and tennis grounds; large, airy rooms; excellent table; piazza on two sides of house; 1 mile from church; raise own vegetables. References on application.

R. P. TAPPEN—Over Brook House. 5 minutes' walk; accommodate 20; adults $5, children $3, transient $1; raise own vegetables; good livery attached; convenient to church; good table; very healthy location; bracing air; no malaria or mosquitoes; good fishing and gunning. References on application.

F. S. WILSON—Homestead-on-the-Hill Farm-house. 1 mile; accommodate 20; adults $5 to $7, children half rate, transient $1; discount to season guests; situated on high and healthy location, commanding a magnificent view of surrounding country; rooms large and cheery; bountiful table; excellent gunning and fishing. References on application.

Mrs. A. A. MORRIS—Adults $6, transient $1. Correspondence solicited.

DRASSER HOUSE.

EPHRAIM N. BAXTER—Farm-house. ¼ mile; accommodate 10; adults $6, transient $1 ; discount to season guests ; good trout-fishing near house; raise own vegetables; good table; excellent livery; picturesque scenery; within one mile of church. References on application.

MAGGIE LIBOLT—Farm-house. Accommodate 18; adults $5.

CENTREVILLE, SULLIVAN CO.

A small village in an agricultural district, 1,146 feet above tidewater. Fine views are here afforded of the Shawangunk and Catskill Mountains and the Neversink Valley.

106 MILES FROM NEW YORK.
FARE $2.40;
EXCURSION, $4.37.

CENTREVILLE STATION—Centreville Station Post-Office.

DAVID ROBINSON—Rose Farm, farm-house, and farm of 100 acres. ¼ mile ; accommodate 25 ; adults $5 to $6 ; discount to season guests ; house has been enlarged and fitted up for every comfort of home ; occupies a high position, commanding a fine view of Shawangunk and Catskill Mountains and the surrounding country for many miles ; excellent fishing and gunning ; boats free of charge ; raise own vegetables ; livery attached ; good table. Correspondence solicited.

J. P. MOORE—Farm-house. 2 miles ; accommodate 30 ; adults $5 to $8, children according to age, transient $1 ; situated on high ground; abundance of shade; large double piazzas; beautiful lawn; magnificent scenery ; large and airy rooms ; new house and new furniture ; every convenience for guests ; liberal table, with abundance of fresh milk and eggs ; raise our own vegetables ; good fishing in Fowlwood and McKee lakes; first-class livery ; 1 mile from church. References on application.

H. L. STURGIS—Farm-house. 1 mile from depot ; adults $5 and $6, children half price ; discount to season guests ; located on high ground ; grand views of the surrounding country ; raise own vegetables ; free transportation to and from depot. Refers to R. McCullough, 337 W. 29th Street, New York.

HORACE M. REXFORD—Farm-house. ¼ mile ; accommodate 10 ; rates on application ; transient $1 ; excellent trout-fishing ; good livery ; fine gunning ; free transportation ; fine table; healthy location ; bracing air ; pure spring water. References on application.

B. AUCHMOODY— Fair View Dairy Farm. 1 mile ; accommodate 15 ; rates on application ; pleasantly situated ; within a short distance of the post-office, church, etc. ; plenty of shade ; ¼ mile from Lake Wood ; good boating, fishing, etc. ; excellent table. References on application.

Mrs. J. B. GARDNER—Prospect Farm House. 1¼ miles ; accommodate 20 ; 10 rooms; terms on application ; free transportation to and from depot ; situated near Lake Wood, affording fine boating, fishing and bathing ; convenient to church ; grand view of Catskill and Shawangunk Mountains and the beautiful Neversink Valley ; 1,600 feet high. References on application.

JAMES A. ATWELL—Farm-house. Accommodate 20 ; adults $5 to $6 ; free transportation ; large, airy rooms ; good beds ; plenty of fresh milk, eggs and vegetables ; ice-cream and chickens; good livery ; first-class table. Best of city references.

THOMAS G. BLACK—Farm-house. 1 mile ; accommodate 15 ; adults $5, children $3, transient $1 ; new house pleasantly situated in a fine location ; good livery ; raise our own vegetables ; 1 mile from church ; good trout and pickerel fishing. References on application.

THOMAS J. KNAPP—Maple Hill Farm House. 2½ miles; accommodate 20 ; adults $5, children $3 ; free transportation ; elevation 1,200 feet above the sea ; large piazza ; plenty of shade ; tennis ; music ; good table ; raise our own vegetables ; excellent fishing, trout brook on the farm. Refers to Wm. B. Penfold, 16 and 18 Reade Street, New York, and E. S. Howe, 53 Downing Street, Brooklyn, N. Y.

Mrs. JAMES CANTHERS—Mountain View Farm House. 2 miles; accommodate 20; adults $5, children $3; free transportation to and from depot; good fishing; first-class livery; house beautifully located on high elevation, with large and airy rooms; good table, liberally supplied with ice-cream, chickens, milk, eggs, etc. City references.

JOHN SENGSTACKEN—Farm-house. 2 miles; accommodate 20; adults $5, children under ten $3, transient $1; plenty of shady trees; splendid views of Catskill Mountains; excellent table; chickens, eggs, ice-cream, etc.; raise own vegetables; good fishing and gunning; own livery. References on application.

Mrs. B. S. HORTON—Farm-house. 1 mile; accommodate 20; rates on application; discount to season guests; pleasantly situated near Lake Wood; plenty of shade; beautiful view of Shawangunk and Catskill Mountains and Neversink Valley; good table; plenty of milk, fresh eggs, etc.; livery attached. Refers to Mrs. L. E. Muller, 10 Charlton Street, New York; Mrs. Lawrence Thompson, 172 Clermont Avenue, Brooklyn, N. Y.

M. D. KNAPP—Farm boarding-house. Accommodate 10. Terms and full particulars on application.

JOHN H. GEIDEMAN—Orchard Farm House. Accommodate 15; adults $5 to $6.

Mrs. A. R. GALBRAITH—Boarding-house. Near station; accommodate 20. Terms and particulars on application.

Mrs. GEORGE A. BROCK—Accommodate 10; adults $6, children $3, transient $1.

DAVID LOGAN—Accommodate 20; adults $5 to $6, children $3.

CENTREVILLE STATION—Glen Wild Post-Office.

EUGENE W. BOWERS—Farm-house. 5 miles; accommodate 30; adults $6 to $8, children reduction, transient $1; discount to season guests; free transportation; excellent fishing and hunting; 1,200 feet above sea-level; cataract near house; good table; large piazza; plenty of shade; no malaria; good roads; charming scenery; own livery; near church. References on application.

CENTREVILLE STATION—Ulster Heights Post-Office.

MICHAEL J. YONKER—Farm-house. 4 miles; accommodate 30; adults $6 to $7, children under ten half price; nice location; 2,500 feet above the sea; fruit trees of all kinds around the house; raise own vegetables; excellent trout-fishing in the Beaverkill; good gunning; free transportation; near to all churches; charming scenery; good table; pure water. References and full particulars on application.

FALLSBURGH, SULLIVAN CO.

108 MILES FROM NEW YORK.
FARE, $2.83;
EXCURSION, $4.85.

The village is 1,224 feet above the sea, and receives its name from the falls of the Neversink river at this point. The main fall is twenty-five feet in height, and the stream is very deep, and dashes through the narrow, rock-bound channel for a long distance below the falls, wearing by its incessant action basin-like cavities in the solid rocks of the river-bed. The region is gaining in popularity each year, and many a tired city merchant and wearied belle find rest and recreation among its many quiet and peaceful homes. The country is unsurpassed in beauty. From lofty hills overlooking rich valleys through which run brooks filled with trout, can be seen here and there beautiful lakes surrounded by cool woods, while green orchards and waving fields of grass and grain meet the eye on every side. Fine drives skirt the river on both banks, and, at a distance of about two miles apart, there

NEVERSINK RIVER—FALLSBURGH.

are thriving villages. The river itself is a succession of cataracts and rapids, with small intervening pools alive with fish. Here there are no mosquitoes, no danger of malarial diseases or hay-fever. The drives are unsurpassed in beauty and variety of the scenery through which they pass, and the roads are excellent. From Fallsburgh, northwest, following the Neversink up to the foot of the "Big Indian," the country is equally beautiful and inviting.

FALLSBURGH STATION—Fallsburgh Post-Office.

Miss K. Murray—Farm-house. 2½ miles; accommodate 20; terms and references on application; free transportation; raise our own vegetables; home comforts. Write for particulars.

P. Vandermark—Farm-house. 1¾ miles; terms on application; house large; grounds well shaded; pleasant drives; daily mails; church and telegraph convenient; perfectly healthy location. References on application.

William Johnson—2 miles; accommodate 25; terms and particulars on application; excellent boating; good fishing; good table; delightful views. Refers to William J. McCready, Old Dominion S. S. Co., 235 West Street, New York; Stephen Cahoone, 18 Wall Street, New York; Dr. B. Andrews, 227 Berkeley Place, Brooklyn, N. Y.

Willard A. Dutcher—Farm-house. 2 miles; accommodate 25; adults $5 to $6. Correspondence solicited.

FALLSBURGH STATION—South Fallsburgh Post-Office.

Albert Pagel—Modern farm-house. 1¼ miles; accommodate 20; rates on application; free transportation; house situated 100 yards from the Neversink river; rooms large and airy, facing south; porch and lawn; plenty of shade; orchard near the house; beautiful views; pure air; clear spring water; farm extends one mile along the river front; excellent and quiet location; raise our own vegetables; good fishing and gunning; good livery. Refers to Mrs. James B. Sheridan, 317 Lenox Avenue, New York; J. F. Werthers, 47 and 49 Liberty Street, New York, and Douglas Sheridan, 32 Nassau Street, New York.

Mrs. Chas. O'Neill—Farm-house. 1 mile; accommodate 20; 12 rooms; terms on application; discount to season guests; free transportation; large, three-story house; spacious piazza; situated on high ground; abundant shade; plenty of milk, cream and eggs; guests can have their own horses boarded on farm at reasonable rates; very healthful, fever never known. References on application.

James Hanlon—Farm and boarding-house. ¼ mile from depot; accommodate 30; telegraph and post-office; every convenience; house pleasantly situated on high ground; home comforts; table abundantly supplied with fruits and vegetables from the farm; good piano, livery, etc. Terms and references on application.

Willard Elmore—Farm-house. 1½ miles; accommodate 20; adults $5 to $6, children under ten years $4, transient $1; free transportation; high, dry and healthful; airy rooms; comfortable beds; views extensive and very fine; plenty of shade; pure air; excellent water; pleasant walks and drives; beautiful lake of nearly 100 acres; fine boating, fishing and bathing; raise our own vegetables. Refers to F. Walker, 14 Maiden Lane, New York; George W. Smith, 161 Willoughby Street, Brooklyn, N. Y.; Edw. Griffith, 433 High Street, Newark, N. J., and Frank Blauvent, 72 E. 115th Street, New York.

M. C. Brome—Large farm-house. 1 mile; accommodate 15; rates on application; house pleasantly situated, within a short distance of Brown's pond; pleasant walks; plenty of shade; large sleeping and connecting rooms; excellent pickerel and bass fishing; good gunning; free transportation; discount to season guests; first-class livery; 1 mile from church; good table; pure water. Refers to R. F. Schorah, 739 De Kalb Ave., Brooklyn, N. Y.

Samuel Durland—Farm-house. 2 miles; accommodate 12; adults $6, children reduction, transient $1; discount to season guests; nicely situated on high knoll; good brook runs through place; stocked with trout, pickerel, perch and bass; excellent well water, and a very fine orchard affording plenty of shade; good croquet grounds. Refers to Edward Long, 15 Wall Street, care of H. B. Howland, New York, and H. B. Johnson, 212 Broadway, care of Knox.

C. E. CONKLIN—Shawangunk Valley House. ¼ mile; accommodate 25; adults $5 and $6; within short distance of Shawangunk Lake; 40 acres of private fish pond on the farm, well stocked with pickerel, perch, cat-fish, etc.; boats and fishing free to guests; good livery at reasonable rates; excellent table; plenty of shade. Refers to B. F. Conklin, Police Headquarters, Brooklyn, N. Y.; Jos. W. Genner, 107 Kosciusko Street, Brooklyn, N. Y.; Mrs. J. D. Walsh, 396 Wythe Avenue, Brooklyn, N. Y.; A. Brand, 54 Sterling Street, Newark, N. J., and Mrs. J. Timoney, 321 E. 19th Street, New York.

JOHN BILLINGS—Farm-house. 1 mile; accommodate 20; adults $5 to $7, no reduction for children; free transportation; raise our own vegetables; abundance of milk, cream, butter and eggs; house well furnished; excellent beds, piano, etc.; large, shady grounds; good livery; fine drives and walks; fishing in vicinity. Being well acquainted in this vicinity, will, if requested, meet parties looking for board, and assist them in procuring suitable places. Refers to Capt. James Whitney, U. S. Army, 113 West 73d Street, New York; Robert Stewart, Manager, Franklin Bank Note Co., New York, and Wm. H. Clark, of Wm. Clark & Sons, Bankers, Tribune Building, New York.

J. W. WHITTAKER—Accommodate 25; adults $5 to $6, children $4. Write for particulars.

ARCHIE D. O'NEILL—Hotel. Within 100 feet of station; accommodate 40; adults $7 to $10, children half, transient $1.50; newly furnished throughout; 25 large and airy rooms; excellent trout, bass, and pickerel fishing; close to post and telegraph; first-class livery attached. References on application.

Mrs. G. A. GRAY—Mountain View Farm House. 1½ miles; accommodate 25; adults $6. Particulars on application.

M. M. CARNEY—Farm-house. 1 mile; accommodate 15; adults $6. Correspondence solicited.

FALLSBURGH STATION—Mongaup Valley Post-Office.

SETH OLMSTED—Hotel. 5 miles; accommodate 20; adults $6 to $8, children half rates, transient $1.25; discount to season guests; near post-office and church; within short distance of four lakes; raise own vegetables; excellent trout-fishing; good partridge, rabbit and woodcock shooting; fine livery; free transportation; good table. References on application.

FALLSBURGH STATION—Grahamsville Post-Office.

Mrs. MICHAEL WALTER—Farm-house. 10 miles; accommodate 16; adults $6, children $2 to $4, transient $1; pure spring water; large rooms; shady piazza; piano in house; raise own vegetables; good trout-fishing; daily mail; convenient to church. References on application. Free transportation.

HULTS SMITH—Farm-house. 9 miles; accommodate 20; adults $5 and $6, children reduction, transient $1; discount to season guests; situated on high ground; plenty of shade; raise own vegetables; good gunning and fishing; good table. References and full particulars on application.

Mrs. AUSTIN PORTER—Farm-house 11 miles; accommodate 20; adults $6; children $3.

C. W. PIERCE—Sycamore House. Accommodate 25. Terms and full particulars on application.

A. B. PORTER—Terms, references and particulars on application.

GEORGE B. REYNOLDS—Private residence. Accommodate 25; terms $6 and $7. Write for particulars.

FALLSBURGH STATION—Maplewood Post-Office.

JOHN HILL—Summer home. 3½ miles; accommodate 30; adults $6, children $4, transient $1; house situated on high ground; abundance of shade; good fishing and hunting; daily mails; good livery accommodations on place. Refers to H. W. Pamphilon, 30 Bond Street, New York, and Francis L. Hine, Astor Place and 8th Street, New York.

DANIEL PARISH—Farm boarding-house. 3 miles; accommodate 20; adults $6 to $8, transient $1.50; first-class table and accommodations; raise our own vegetables; 3 miles to church; daily mail; charming surroundings.

Mrs. O. ROBINSON—Hillside Cottage. Adults $6, children $3. Write for particulars.

FALLSBURGH STATION—Thompsonville Post-Office.

CYRUS RUMSEY—Farm-house. 2 miles; accommodate 25; adults $5 to $7, reduced rates for children, transient $1.50; free transportation; discount to season guests; trout brook on farm, also good bass and pickerel fishing; 1 mile from church; raise our own vegetables; good gunning —foxes, rabbit, quail and pheasant; splendid scenery; romantic walks and drives.

JOHN H. SCOTT—Farm-house. 2½ miles; accommodate 16; adults $6.

FALLSBURGH STATION—Hasbrouck Post-Office.

HARDENBERGH HOMESTEAD—Farm-house. 1,500 feet above sea-level; 6 miles, over fine road, with beautiful scenery; accommodate 40; adults $7 to $9, children not desired, $6 per week if taken, transient $1.50; pleasantly situated; well furnished; hot and cold water bath on second floor; running spring water; bowling-alley and dancing-floor on place; shady ground; plenty of milk, eggs and fruit; raise own vegetables; good fishing and gunning. For particulars, before July 1st, inquire Hardenbergh, at 400 W. 57th Street, New York; after July, at above address.

Mrs. E. D. GILLETT—Farm boarding-house. 7 miles; accommodate 20; adults $5 to $7, children half rates.

GEORGE H. CROSS—Accommodate 12. Particulars on application.

FALLSBURGH STATION—Bridgeville Post-Office.

S. H. DECKER—Echo Dale Farm House. 5 miles; accommodate 10; free transportation; large piazza; house on elevation; grove and river near by; ½ mile to church and post-office; daily mail; pure water. Rates and references given on application.

ALFRED M. HOYT—Farm-house. 5 miles; accommodate 12; adults $5, children $3, transient 75 cents; good fishing in the Neversink river; free transportation; liberal table; ample shade; healthy location; fine walks and drives. References on application.

Mrs. AUSTIN RACE—Farm-house. 4 miles; accommodate 10; adults $5, children $3, transient 75 cents; discount to season guests; free transportation one way; raise our own vegetables; excellent fishing in lake and river—whitefish, trout, pickerel; no charge for boats; good gunning —partridge, rabbit and squirrel; good livery; convenient to church.

Mrs. O. ROBINSON (Maplewood Post-Office)—Hillside Cottage. Adults $6, children $3. Write for particulars.

WOODBOURNE, SULLIVAN CO.

Four miles from Fallsburgh Station, over an excellent road and at an elevation of 1,400 feet above the sea, is located this delightful summer retreat. The scenery is superb, and the views up and down the valley are of unsurpassed loveliness. The Neversink river, on which the village is situated, is pronounced one of the best trout streams in the State. The surrounding country abounds in mountains, forests, streams and lakes. East Lake, on the summit of one of the many highlands of Sullivan County, completely surrounded by forests, affords ample sport for boating and fishing. This beautiful sheet of water is within easy access of the village, and is a popular resort for picnics, etc. There are other lakes within a few miles of this resort, accessible by excellent drives, among which are Pleasant Lake, Loch Sheldrake, Alton Lake and White Lake. Aside from the delightful scenery and well-kept roads of this locality, it is a fact- which the experience of years has demonstrated, that the air circulating among the hills and valleys is possessed of curative properties that render the existence of pulmonary or bronchial difficulties next to an impossibility. The value of this region for cool, dry air and pure spring water is now recognized by leading physicians and tourists who, having once visited this resort, are certain to return for many successive seasons.

NEVERSINK RIVER AT WOODBOURNE.

FALLSBURGH STATION—Woodbourne Post-Office.

JOHN MURPHY—Pleasant View House. 2½ miles; accommodate 100; adults $7 to $8, children under ten half, transient $1.50 per day; discount to season guests; transportation, adults 50 cents, children 25 cents; has all the attractions of a summer home; situated on a farm of 200 acres; the culinary department cannot be surpassed; elevation 2,000 feet above tidewater, commanding a fine view of the Catskill, Shawangunk and Walnut Mountains; daily mail; telegraph and telephone convenient; excellent tennis court. Refers to J. Y. Watkins, 16 Catharine Street, New York; Dr. Conner, 60 Court Street, Brooklyn, N. Y., and J. S. McCarthy, 84 Bowery, New York.

L. L. WALDORF—Woodbourne House. 4 miles; accommodate 80; adults $7 to $10, children under ten $4, transient $1.50; free transportation; excellent livery accommodation; delightfully dry, cool air; no malaria; large, airy rooms and best of beds; first-class table; mountain spring water; perfect sanitary regulations; plenty of shade; large, pleasant piazza; fishing, boating and hunting; tennis, etc.; daily mails, telegraph, and churches; send for circular. Refers to Chas. Ford, 160 Chambers Street, Superintendent New York Hospital; Dr. Jean F. Chauveau, Jr., 31 W. 60th Street, New York, and Mrs. C. V. Dix, 93 St. Mark's Avenue, Brooklyn, N. Y.

SILAS MERRITT—Farm boarding-house. 3½ miles; accommodate 65; rates on application; transient $1.25; house newly furnished; large, airy rooms; large piazza; bath-room; running spring water; shady grounds; pleasant drives; telephone and telegraph near by; no malaria or mosquitoes; trout and pickerel fishing; boating and bathing; accommodations for horses and carriages; good livery accommodations; croquet and lawn tennis. Refers to E. C. Gedney, 228 and 230 Greenwich Street, New York; J. A. Williams, 50 Wall Street, New York; Wm. Beneki, 199 Canal Street, New York.

JAMES N. STILLWELL—Ridge Farm House. 2½ miles; accommodate 15; terms on application; discount to season guests; free transportation; 2 miles from church. Refers to John Watts, 113 South 5th Street, Brooklyn, E. D., and D. S. Gerehart, 379 State Street, Brooklyn, N. Y. Correspondence solicited.

M. EIDEL—Farm-house. 4 miles; accommodate 25; adults $6 to $7; free transportation; house situated on the banks of the Neversink; raise our own vegetables; boats free to guests; dancing-pavilion half a mile above village; driving-park; extensive shady grounds; excellent livery; convenient to church. Refers to Mrs. M. Skelly, 560 Carlton Avenue, Brooklyn, N. Y.; J. Metz, 130 E. 70th Street, New York; John P. Yank, 420 E. 84th Street, New York.

MARTIN MERRITT—Neversink View Farm House. 5 miles; accommodate 35; adults $6 to $8; situated on the banks of the Neversink river; large, airy rooms; excellent beds; spacious piazza; raise our own vegetables; bountiful table; fresh butter, milk and eggs. References on application.

MADISON MERRITT—Farm-house. 6 miles; accommodate 20; adults $6, children $3; free transportation; large rooms; piano; broad piazza; raise own vegetables; good trout-fishing in Neversink river; good table. New York and Brooklyn references on application.

ABNER MERRITT—Neversink Valley Farm House. 4 miles; accommodate 20; adults $6 to $7, children $5, transient $1; discount to season guests; raise own vegetables; good table; pleasant walks and drives; excellent trout-fishing. References and full particulars on application.

W. T. KINNEY—Farm-house. 5 miles; accommodate 30; adults $6 to $7, children under ten $3; situated on the banks of the Neversink; large lawn; plenty of shade; double piazza; good table; large pleasant rooms; free transportation; raise own vegetables; good livery. References on application.

DARIUS DEPUY—Farm boarding-house. 6 miles; accommodate 25; adults $6, children $3, transient $1; have a large farm and dairy; plenty of milk, eggs, poultry, etc.; pure water; bracing mountain air; have a summer pavilion for dancing, and a lake for boating and bathing; good trout-fishing; first-class gunning; small trout stream on farm; discount to season guests; raise own vegetables; free transportation. Refers to W. S. Paryborn, 815 Quincy Street, Brooklyn, N. Y.; Dr. J. Corbin, 651 Hancock Street, Brooklyn, N. Y.; Chas. F. Carlock, 265 W. 131st Street, New York City.

MRS. H. LOCKWOOD—Private residence. 4 miles; accommodate 12. Rates and references on application.

BENJAMIN VERNOOY—Boarding-house. 4 miles ; accommodate 25 ; adults $7 to $10, children $4 to $6, transient $1.50; five minutes' walk from church, post-office, stores, etc. ; nice drives ; plenty of shade ; pleasant rambles through the woodlands ; raise own vegetables ; croquet and lawn tennis ; excellent trout-fishing ; good gunning ; first-class livery. Refers to Jacob Masten, Charles E. Bebee, James H. Bartlett, all with Teft, Weller & Co., 330 Broadway, New York.

WILLIAM J. TODD—Accommodate 30. Terms moderate. Correspondence solicited.

C. E. STEVENS—Woodbine Cottage. Opens June 15th, 1892. Correspondence solicited.

Mrs. FRANK SMITH—Farm-house. 7 miles ; accommodate 10 ; adults $5 to $6. Send for particulars.

Mrs. C. E. STEVENS—Private residence, Woodbine Cottage. Open June 1st ; fine healthy location ; romantic walks and drives ; good table ; comfortable rooms ; good fishing ; pure spring water ; home comforts ; high ground, commanding fine views of surrounding country. For references and further particulars, address P. O. B. 106.

JAMES OSTERHOUT—Boarding-house. 4 miles ; accommodate 50 ; adults $7 to $10, children $4 to $6, transient $1.50 ; discount to season guests ; excellent table ; pure spring water throughout the house ; 100 feet of wide piazza ; plenty of shade ; pleasant drives and walks ; good livery at moderate rates ; raise our own vegetables ; boating and fishing on the Neversink ; daily mail ; telegraph ; churches. References on application.

MONTICELLO, SULLIVAN CO.

Connections via Fallsburgh, and Stage Line Five Miles Over Toll Roads.
Stages Meet All Trains.

Here, 1,500 feet above the ocean, is one of the most charming villages in the State. The village itself is on rolling land, and its residences and private grounds are extremely attractive. High hills rise on every side, from which extensive views of the rugged outlying country may be enjoyed. The atmosphere is pure and bracing, and fevers of any kind never originate in this region. The air is peculiarly favorable to asthmatics and persons afflicted with kindred diseases. A mosquito would be a curiosity in this section. Heat never interferes with sleep, and neither dampness nor fog render evening or morning disagreeable.

126 MILES FROM NEW YORK.
LOCAL FARE, LIMITED, $3.00;
EXCURSION, $5.00.

There are trout streams in the vicinity, and the best of bass-fishing in Pleasant Lake, a beautiful sheet of water, one mile distant. Katrina Falls, a picturesque cataract, with good surroundings ; Edward's Island, in the Neversink, and Strange's Grove are favorite retreats about the village. Besides the unsurpassed fishing found in the vicinity of Monticello, the autumn season brings abundance of game, partridge and other small game being especially plentiful. The churches of the village are an Episcopal, a Methodist, a Presbyterian and a Catholic.

MONTICELLO & FALLSBURGH TALLY-HO STAGE LINE. A line of coaches between Monticello and Fallsburgh will commence running June 15, 1892, and meet all N. Y., O. and W. passenger-trains, except the night line (Nos. 5 and 6). The proprietor having an extensive connection, and being well known throughout the locality, will be pleased to assist those in search of desirable summer homes in procuring suitable accommodation. Ticket and Stage Office at Rockwell Building, Monticello, N. Y. Private carriages furnished at reasonable rates. Charles Stanton, proprietor.

PLEASANT LAKE.

MANSION HOUSE.

FALLSBURGH STATION—Monticello Post-Office.

Mrs. LeGrand Morris—Mansion House, family hotel. Accommodate 100; adults $8 to $12. according to rooms, children according to age, transient $2.50; special terms for families; numerous cottages lodge our surplus guests; vegetables fresh from the garden every day; we have families who have spent the summer with us regularly for twenty years; our table is unsurpassed; roads, drives and scenery unexcelled; pure spring water; excellent livery attached to the house; Sullivan County is the sanitarium of the State, and is highly recommended by physicians; excellent fishing; good gunning—fox, bear and deer. References: National Union Bank, Monticello, N. Y., or any of the Supervisors of the county.

Mrs. R. B. Towner—Towner Villa, boarding-house. Accommodate 30; adults $8 to $12, children half price, transient $2; discount to season guests; beautifully situated at the head of Main Street, commanding a fine view of the town and surrounding country; large lawn affording plenty of shade; fine grove in the rear of house; established over twenty-five years; first-class livery; five minutes' walk from churches. References and full particulars on application.

Mrs. Fannie Curley—Curley's Hotel, hotel and boarding-house. Accommodate 35; adults $6 to $8, children $3 to $5, transient $1.50; discount to season guests; situated near the village park and county buildings; have a grand view of many mountains for miles around; good bass, pickerel, perch and trout fishing; raise own vegetables; good fox and duck shooting; livery connected with house. Refers to M. Doran, 205 E. 121st Street, New York; James H. Sheils, 234 Clinton Street, New York.

Charles Burnham—Boarding-house. Accommodate 30; adults $8 and $10; situated in the centre of village on high ground; pleasant rooms; lawn tennis and croquet grounds; fine lawn; good shade; accommodation for horses; romantic walks and drives; excellent table; pure spring water. References and full particulars on application.

Mrs. C. Bolsom—Hotel and boarding-house. Accommodate 50; 30 sleeping-rooms; adults $5 to $8, transient $1; discount to season guests; excellent fishing; good gunning; house fronts on Main Street; good livery attached; first-class table; romantic walks and drives; pure spring water; charming scenery; home comforts; healthy location. Refers to Henry I. Primsoll, 12 Clinton Place, New York, or 32 Tompkins Place, Brooklyn, E. D., N. Y.

JOHN HAGAN—Farm-house. Accommodate 20 ; adults $5 and $6, children $4, transient $1 ; discount to season guests; raise own vegetables; good fishing and gunning ; boats and fishing-tackle at moderate rate; pleasantly situated on high ground, commanding a fine view of the surrounding country; healthy location : excellent table ; bracing air ; pure spring water; good livery; excellent roads. References on application.

J. G. & M. A. MITCHELL—"The" Mitchell House, with accommodation for 80 guests ; situated on the highest ground in Monticello, with an altitude of 1,540 feet; has large lawns for lawn tennis and croquet; is only two blocks from post-office; rooms are large and airy with high ceilings, also two music-rooms and a very large dining-room, which is used as an amusement hall in the evening; fresh vegetables; butter and eggs always supplied. Rates, references and information on application.

HOTEL ROCKWELL.

GEORGE W. ROCKWELL, JR., Proprietor—Hotel Rockwell. Comfortably accommodate 100 ; situated exactly in the centre of the village, opposite the park (see cut of same), where evening band concerts are given weekly ; less than one minute's walk to post-office, telegraph and bank ; convenient to church ; the Monticello and Fallsburgh stage line stops at the door ; hotel provided with bath-rooms, water-closets, steam, gas, and modern conveniences generally ; fine amusement hall; spacious piazzas ; ample shade ; first-class livery connected with house ; especial attention will be given to parties coming into the country early in search of location for season ; comfortable quarters always reserved for transient guests. Best of references. Circulars furnished on application.

Mrs. E. W. EVANS—Private residence. Accommodate 12; adults $7, children $3.50; large, pleasant rooms ; excellent table; plenty of shade; pleasant and healthy location; raise own vegetables ; nice spring water; within four blocks of post-office; romantic walks and drives; first-class livery; good roads. References and full particulars on application.

Mrs. M. C. WHEELER—Boarding-house. Accommodate 30; adults $7 to $10, no children, transient. $2; fine views; best hair-beds and spring-mattresses; first-class table; pleasant walks; home cooking; raise own vegetables; good trout, bass and pickerel fishing; all kinds of game; first-class livery; very near all churches; pleasant situation; picturesque scenery; ample shade. References exchanged.

STEPHEN A. REYNOLDS—Summer cottage. Accommodate 40; tenth season; terms on application; house situated on high ground on one of the most pleasant streets in the village; near to post-office, churches, telegraph and telephone offices; large, airy rooms, neatly furnished, all opening into hall, and made connecting if desired; large shaded lawn; double piazza; table well supplied with everything in season. We aim to please our guests; references on application.

HIRAM TOWNER—Boarding-house. Accommodate 50; adults $9, children $6, transient $2. This delightful summer resort, situated on high, sightly ground, is newly furnished for the accommodation of summer guests; horses and carriages and saddle horses to be had on the premises; good gunning and fishing; very healthy; pure spring water; bracing air; romantic walks and drives; excellent table. References on application; write for further particulars.

RICHARD BEBEE—Mongaup Heights Farm-House. Accommodate 20; adults $6, children $3, transient $1; discount to season guests; free transportation; raise our own vegetables; splendid view of the surrounding country; excellent fishing in White Lake, Pleasant Lake and Mongaup river; splendid gunning of all kinds; 2 miles from church. Refers to Cornelius Evans, 28 Platt Street, New York; J. J. Farley, 314 E. 12th Street, New York; Walter Mabie, 12 Laidlaw Avenue, Jersey City, N. J.

W. R. HAGAN—Prospect House. Accommodate 50; adults $7 to $9, reduction to children; house is one minute's walk to Pleasant Lake; boats at reasonable rates; fine roads for driving and bicycling; good table and comfortable beds; location healthful and pleasant; airy rooms on second and third floors; raise our own vegetables; good gunning and fishing; first-class livery. References on application.

Mrs. OWEN LEWIS—The Saginaw Farm House. Rates furnished on application; raise our own vegetables; good boating and fishing; boats free to guests; excellent gunning; 1 mile from church; location of house unsurpassed for beauty and natural scenery; excellent table; private conveyance; pure spring water; charming surroundings; good airy rooms; liberal table; romantic walks and drives; home comforts. References and full particulars on application.

J. H. MILLSPAUGH—Lake View Cottage. Accommodate 40; adults $7 to $10, children $5, transient $1.50; house overlooking Pleasant Lake; pleasant shade; 75 feet of piazza; boats furnished at reasonable rates; excellent pickerel and bass fishing. References on application.

JOSEPH L. REYNOLDS—Boarding-house. Accommodate 20; adults $6 to $8, no children, transient $1.50; situated on a pleasant street in the village; free from malaria; good roads and pleasant walks; good fishing; raise own vegetables; fresh milk; good table; piano for guests; croquet ground. References exchanged. Lock box 27.

ROBERT K. BRADLEY—Boarding-house. ¼ mile; accommodate 15; adults $7, children $3.50; good fishing and hunting; church opposite the house; healthy location; beautiful drives; raise our own vegetables; good livery accommodations. References on application.

JAMES H. TAYLOR—Pleasant Lake Farm and Boarding-house. 2½ miles; accommodate 30; adults $7 to 8, transient $1.50; a fine view of the lake from the house; raise our own vegetables; good trout, bass and pickerel fishing; boats free to guests; good gunning for small game; first-class livery; free transportation to and from depot. References on application.

E. F. THOMPSON—Farm-house. Accommodate 15; adults $6, children $3; good fishing and gunning; raise own vegetables; 1 mile from church; pleasantly located; comfortable rooms; pure air; spring water; first-class table; charming walks and drives. References on application.

TO RENT.

Mrs. THORNTON A. NIVEN—"The Daisy" Cottage. Furnished house to rent for season or longer, with or without stable; 11 rooms; ample closets and bath-room; newly fitted and furnished; next door to St. John's Church; two minutes' walk to post-office, telegraph, hotels and park. Photograph and plan of cottage furnished if desired; personal inspection preferred.

MONGAUP RIVER, NEAR HURLEYVILLE.

PARK, MONTICELLO.

GEORGE McLOUGHLIN—Farm-house. Accommodate 12 ; adults $8, transient $1.50 ; large, roomy house; situated on very high ground, commanding fine views in every direction; spacious, shady yard; first-class table; raise own vegetables; good shooting; stabling for horses; 1½ miles from church ; romantic walks and drives ; good roads ; comfortable rooms. Refers to H. H. Brown, 56 Wall Street, New York.

Mrs. MARY E. STAGE—Accommodate 25; adults $5 to $8, children $4 to $5. References exchanged.

A. R. CRANDALL—Village residence. Accommodate 18 ; terms $7, $8 and $10.

INTER LACHEN COTTAGE—Box 7, Monticello; accommodate 30; adults $7 to $12, no children, transient $2.

WILLIAM BRICE—Edgewood Farm House. Accommodate 10; adults $7. Correspondence solicited.

Mrs. ISAAC O. SMITH—Private boarding-house ; accommodate 14 ; adults $7, transient $1.50.

W. L. WILLETS—Farm-house. Accommodate 15 ; adults $6, children reduction, transient $1.

Mrs. C. S. STARR—Village residence. Accommodate 25 ; adults $7 to $10, children rates on application, transient $1.50.

J. C. DE LANEY—Farm-house. Accommodate 13 ; adults $5 to $6, children half rates.

M. A. HALEY—Farm-house. Accommodate 25; adults $5 to $7, children half rate, transient $1.50.

ANDREW W. HALEY—Farm-house. Accommodate 25 ; adults $5 to $7, children half, transient $1.50.

MARTIN TOOHEY—Mountain Spring Farm House. Accommodate 40 ; adults $6 to $7, children reduction.

SENECA DUTCHER—Private house. Accommodate 15 ; adults $7, no children. Write for particulars.

Mrs. P. M. AVERY—Farm-house. Accommodate 10 ; adults $6, children half, transient $1.

JOHN CARPENTER—Private house. Terms and full particulars on application.

A. E. GILLESPIE—Commercial Hotel. Accommodate 40 ; adults $5 to $7. Write for particulars.

Mrs. SETH H. ROYCE—Locust Wood Villa. Accommodate 20. Terms and full particulars on application.

J. J. TROWBRIDGE—Mountain View Summer Home. Accommodate 30 ; adults $6 to $8, children reduction, transient $1.50.

GEORGE W. DECKER—Highland House. Accommodate 30 ; adults $7 to $10, children reduction.

CHARLES ENNIS—Hillside Cottage. Accommodate 12. Rates and references on application.

Miss M. A. WHITTAKER—Boarding-house. Accommodate 15. Terms and full particulars on application.

GEORGE ZIMMERMAN—Maplewood Grove House. The house and grounds are situated on Liberty Street, Monticello ; five minutes' walk from post-office ; beautifully shaded lawns; barn and carriage-house; fine views from the grounds of Pleasant Lake and the surrounding country, none superior in the State. References and full particulars on application.

HURLEYVILLE, SULLIVAN CO.

An important milk station, situated 1,320 feet above the sea. The fishing and hunting are excellent. Very many of the best farm-houses of this section are open for the reception of summer boarders.

111 MILES FROM NEW YORK.
FARE, $2.67;
EXCURSION, $4.73.

HURLEYVILLE STATION—Hurleyville Post-Office.

Mrs. CHARLES T. MISNER—Boarding-house. ¼ mile ; accommodate 10; adults $5 to $6, children $3, transient $1 per day; raise our own vegetables; fine grove in yard at side of house ; good fishing in Loch Sheldrake; good partridge-shooting ; first-class livery close at hand; fresh milk and eggs: romantic surroundings; good table; ¼ mile from church ; nice grove and fine yard. References and full particulars on application.

MONGAUP RIVER.

ROBT. A. HALL—Farm-house. 3 miles; accommodate 20; adults $5 to $6 according to rooms, children $3, transient $1; discount to season guests; families preferred; vegetables raised on farm; good gunning and fishing; near Pleasant and Clear lakes; boats may be had at moderate rates; all kinds of game; good livery. Refers to James Carroher, Sheriff's Office, New York; H. Gerdes, 11 W. 3d Street, New York.

HIRAM HEWLETT—Farm-house. Accommodate 15; adults $5 to $5, children $4, transient $1; raise own vegetables; good fishing; fish-pond within five rods; boats provided; free transportation; good table; very healthy; romantic scenery. References on application.

JOHN WOOD—Maple Hill Farm House. 2 miles; accommodate 20; adults $5 to $6, children $5, transient $1; discount to season guests; house on high ground; plenty of shade; free transportation in our own conveyance; good table; pure water. References and full particulars on application.

F. E. LINDSLEY—Farm-house. 1 mile; accommodate 30; adults $5 to $6, children $4, transient $1; discount to families; good livery; high situation; fine scenery; double piazza; ample shade; spring-beds; piano, spring water; pure milk; fresh eggs, chickens, ice-cream, etc.; laundry; house opens June 1st; free transportation. References on application.

JOSEPH H. WORDEN—Farm-house. Accommodate 35; 2 miles; adults $5 to $6, children $3, transient $1; discount to season guests; raise own vegetables; free transportation; good table; pure spring water; home comforts. References and full particulars on application.

D. H. MITTEER—Farm-house. 1 mile; accommodate 25; adults $5 to $6, children $3, transient $1 per day; discount to season guests; free transportation; fresh mountain air; good water; plenty of shade; raise our own vegetables; excellent table; romantic walks and drives; first-class livery. References on application.

CHARLES MAWER—Thistle Farm House. 3 miles; accommodate 20; adults $5 to $6 per week, children $3, transient $1; discount to season guests; free transportation; house pleasantly situated; home comforts; raise our own vegetables; good table; plenty of milk; shady grounds; large, airy rooms; very healthy location; piano; daily mail. References on application.

W. H. WRIGHT—Farm-house. 1 mile; accommodate 12; adults $5, children $3; good fishing and gunning; house pleasantly situated; large airy rooms; pure spring water; raise own vegetables; 1 mile from church; good table; charming scenery. References and full particulars on application.

JOSEPH S. KILE—Farm-house. ½ mile; accommodate 30; adults $5, children $5; good fishing; bracing mountain air; liberal table, supplied with products of farm; home comforts; romantic walks and drives. Correspondence solicited; references on application.

MARSHALL N. SMITH—Hilldale Boarding-house, with farm attached. 2 miles; accommodate 40; adults $5 to $7, children $5; discount to season guests; free transportation; good fishing and gunning; boats free to guests; first-class livery; raise our own vegetables; ¼ mile from Gray Rock Point; ¼ mile from Sulphur Springs. References on application.

GEORGE BROPHY—Farm-house. 1¼ miles; accommodate 50; adults $5 to $6, children $3; free transportation; large farm-house, situated on high ground; shady walks; boating and fishing within reasonable distance; raise our own vegetables; good fishing and gunning; first-class livery attached; single and double rigs. References on application.

JAMES M. PURVIS—Farm-house. 2 miles; accommodate 35; adults $5 to $6, transient $1; free transportation; raise our own vegetables; good gunning and fishing; 2 miles from church; liberal table; charming walks and drives; bracing mountain air. Refers to Garret Le Roy, Loch Sheldrake, N. Y. Circulars with good references from New York and Brooklyn furnished on application.

WILLIAM A. FOSTER—Pleasant rooms for a party who board themselves.

J. E. DECKER—Has furnished house to rent. Particulars on application.

T. H. SMITH—Accommodate 20; adults $5 to $6, children $5, transient $1.

Mrs. J. W. STICKLE—Will take boarders. Write for terms and full information.

HURLEYVILLE STATION—Woodbourne Post-Office.

JAMES P. SMITH—Echo Hill Farm House. 4 miles; accommodate 20; adults $5 to $6, transient $1; plenty of eggs, fresh meat, poultry, milk and choice butter; livery reasonable; ample shade; pleasant surroundings; very healthy. Reference: J. H. Powell, 29 Stirling Street. Newark, N. J.

HURLEYVILLE STATION—Loch Sheldrake Post-Office.

EDWARD MISNER—Hotel and boarding-house. 2 miles; accommodate 75; adults $6 and $7, children $4, transient $1; good fishing within one hundred feet of house, in Sheldrake Lake—bass, salmon-trout, pickerel; good gunning—partridge, rabbit and woodcock in season; good livery; five minutes' walk to church; house situated on the banks of the Sheldrake Lake of clear spring water; nice, airy rooms; one of the finest places for pleasure-seekers in Sullivan County; will try to do all for the comfort of guests. Refers to D. H. Roche, 45 Second Place, Brooklyn, N. Y.

REXFORD & GARDNER—Boarding-house. 3 miles; accommodate 30; adults $6 and $7, children $5, transient $1; discount to season guests; good fishing; raise own vegetables; have own livery; convenient to church. Full particulars and circular on application.

JOHN H. DIVINE—Cottage. Accommodate 40; ½ mile; adults $5 to $7; finest cottage on lake; observatory 90 feet above water-level; fine roads; good livery; fishing and hunting; short distance to two churches; steamboat on lake. Correspondence solicited.

GARRET LE ROY—Farm-house. 2 miles; accommodate 60; adults $5 to $6, children $5, transient $1; discount to season guests; free transportation; provide boats; own livery; near church; raise our own vegetables. Refers to F. W. White, 40 Leonard Street, New York.

P. E. CODDINGTON—Farm-house. 3 miles; accommodate 16; raise our own vegetables; ½ mile from lake and church; located on high ground; cool breeze; plenty of shade; boating and fishing; daily mail. Rates, references and full particulars on application.

JAMES GRAY—Farm-house. 3 miles; accommodate 20; adults $6, children $4. Write for particulars.

NEAL VAN BINSCHOTEN HOMESTEAD—Reasonable rates. Write for particulars.

HURLEYVILLE STATION—Divine's Corners Post-Office.

JOHN T. CURTIS—Farm-house. 4 miles; accommodate 50; adults $6, children half price, transient $1 per day; good livery; free transportation one way; fine maple grove; splendid strolls; grand scenery; plenty of dancing in the neighborhood; finest well water coming from the spring; raise own vegetables; good trout-fishing; first-class table; home comforts. References and full particulars cheerfully furnished on application.

THOMAS LAWRENCE—Farm-house. 4 miles; accommodate 20; adults $5 to $6, children under ten years half; free transportation in our own conveyance; house located on high ground; large, commodious platform for the accommodation of those wishing to dance; raise our own vegetables; good fishing and gunning. References on application.

BENJAMIN TERWILLIGER—Wintergreen Hill Farm House. 4 miles; accommodate 20; adults $5 to $6, children under ten $4; discount to season guests; free transportation; nicely located; pleasant rooms, high ceilings; few minutes' walk to the hill, which affords a magnificent view of the surrounding country; raise our own vegetables; good fishing and gunning; daily mails. References on application.

M. E. HOBBY—Farm-house. 4 miles; accommodate 30; adults $5 to $6, children $3, transient $1; discount to season guests; free transportation from depot; good gunning and fishing; game of all kinds; first-class livery; high elevation; large, airy rooms; well located in the centre of the village; fine views, plenty of shade; 70 feet of piazza; the best of water; piano; daily mail; fresh milk and eggs; beautiful walks and drives; excellent table; post-office and churches near by. Refers to J. H. Hobby & Son, 286 South Street, New York; Henry A. Hoyt, 54 Pine Street, New York, and J. Harris, of Harris & Kingsley, 132 E. 30th Street, New York.

A. J. CODDINGTON—Farm-house. 4½ miles; accommodate 10; adults $5, children according to age; daily mail; five minutes' walk to post-office; liberal table; beautiful scenery; pure spring water; free transportation. Write for particulars; references on application.

JAMES A. ROOSA—Farm-house. 4 miles; accommodate 25; adults $5 to $6, children $3, transient $1; bracing mountain air; home privileges for all; children welcome; no style; good gunning and fishing; first-class livery; raise own vegetables; free transportation. References on application.

PETER H. ELLER—Farm-house. 4 miles; accommodate 20; adults $5.

LOCH SHELDRAKE.

LIBERTY FALLS, SULLIVAN CO.

> 117 MILES FROM NEW YORK.
> FARE, $2.85;
> EXCURSION, $5.00.

At this point the road crosses the valley of the east branch of the Mongaup river on a new and handsome iron bridge, 102 feet above the water and 1,100 feet long. The scenery is wild and grand, but the falls are traditional, or belong to a former condition of the Mongaup river. The valley of this branch of the Mongaup is not as impressive as that of the Neversink, but is more primitive in its wildness. The village is small but enterprising. The hotels and farm-houses in this vicinity can accommodate about 450 persons at one time, and offer good board at reasonable rates.

LIBERTY FALLS STATION—Liberty Falls Post-Office.

H. M. STODDARD—Accommodate 35; adults $6, no reduction for children; raise our own vegetables; pleasantly situated; forty rods from lake; the fishing in the lake is unsurpassed by any in the country; excellent table; bracing air; pure water; ample shade; large, airy rooms. Full particulars furnished on application. Refers to William Herron & Co., 361 Greenwich Street, New York.

D. J. HAND—Farm-house. 1 mile; accommodate 15; adults $5 to $7, children $4; discount to season guests; free transportation to and from trains; pure water; plenty of vegetables, eggs, milk and butter supplied from our own farm and dairy; excellent roads; daily mail; convenient to telegraph-office; pleasantly situated on high ground; a desirable resort for rest, recreation and health. References exchanged.

E. A. GREGORY—Farm-house. 2 miles; accommodate 20; adults $5 to $6, children half rates, transient $1; discount to season guests; good gunning and fishing; Mongaup stream runs through farm; well stocked with trout, bass and pickerel; boats and fishing-tackle to hire; good livery; shady grounds; long piazza; music; games; daily mail; vegetables, milk, fruit, ice, etc. References on application.

Mrs. S. CARR—Farm-house. 3 miles; accommodate 15; adults $5, children $3; plenty of milk, vegetables and ice-cream; free transportation. Refers to S. B. Baker, Pier 20 East river, New York. Full particulars on application.

JAMES F. PRINCE—Farm-house. 3½ miles; accommodate 15; adults $5, children $2.50, transient $1; good gunning and fishing—all kinds of game; short distance from church; free transportation; plenty of shade; good table; raise own vegetables. Refers to Charles MacDonald, 150 W. 78th Street, New York; Wm. Baldwin, 150 Fifth Avenue, New York.

EDWARD KEOGH—Farm-house. 3 miles; accommodate 25; adults $6 and $7, transient $1; discount to season guests; free transportation; raise our own vegetables; good pickerel and trout fishing; three miles from Catholic church and 1½ from Protestant; healthy location; liberal table; bracing air; charming walks and drives. Write for further particulars.

ELMER E. RHODES—Ridge End Farm Boarding-house, seventh season. Accommodate 30; adults $6; shady grounds; lawn tennis; excellent fishing—trout streams 40 rods from house; plenty of milk and ice; good livery. References and full particulars on application.

GEO. S. SANFORD—Farm-house. 2 miles; free transportation to and from station; situated on high ground; views for miles each way; long front piazza; cottage on farm; good trout-fishing in Mongaup stream, running through the farm, and pickerel in Stevens Lake; will strive to please guests; good livery; daily mail; music; croquet; pure, bracing air and good water.

JOHN CLEMENTS—Farm-house. ¾ mile; accommodate 35; guests taken to and from the depot free of charge; house pleasantly situated on the main road between Liberty and Liberty Falls, commanding a very fine view of the surrounding country; table liberally supplied with fresh vegetables, eggs, milk and good butter. Terms, references and descriptive circular on application.

Mrs. W. W. BARTHOLOMEW—Trout Brook Farm House. ½ mile; accommodate 20. Terms reasonable.

M. N. MIDDAUGH—Farm-house. ¼ mile; accommodate 16; adults $6, children $4, transient $1; discount to season guests; free transportation; good fishing, a trout brook running through the farm; good gunning; first-class livery accommodation; ample shade; romantic walks; pleasant surroundings. References on application. Would rent the house from June 1st at reasonable rate.

Mrs. W. K. LODER—Farm-house. Accommodate 20; adults $5, children $3, transient $1.

HENRY GURD—Farm-house. Accommodate 25; adults $5 to $6, transient $1.

JOHN O. CRUMLEY (Bushville Post-Office)—Farm-house. Accommodate 20. Terms and full particulars on application.

STEVENSVILLE, SULLIVAN CO.

A charming little village, three miles from Liberty Station and five miles from White Lake. The village is situated 1,440 feet above the sea, on the outlet of Stevensville Lake, a beautiful sheet of water three and a half miles long. The country surrounding is exceedingly attractive and healthful. The lake affords excellent opportunities for boating and fishing. Many of the best farm-houses in this vicinity are open for the reception of summer guests.

[LIMITED FARE. EXCURSION.]

LIBERTY FALLS STATION—Stevensville Post-Office.

W. H. SANFORD—Farm-house. 2½ miles; 12 rooms; adults $5, children $3, transient $1; free transportation to and from station; we strive to please our guests; plenty of shade; front porch 64 feet long; trout and pickerel fishing in Mongaup river and Stevensville Lake; boats free to guests; good gunning; 6 miles from White Lake, 8 miles from Monticello; good livery; one mile to church. Refers to Mrs. Dr. S. A. Harris, 133 West 127th Street, New York, and De Groot Bros, 112 Greenpoint Avenue, Brooklyn.

A cottage to rent, in good order, with plenty of shade, pure water and ground for garden. Apply to W. H. Sanford, Stevensville, N. Y.

J. W. SANFORD—Farm-house. 3 miles; accommodate 16; adults $5 to $6, children $3, transient $1; raise own vegetables; good fishing; fine views; cool breezes; pure spring water; ample shade; pleasant walks; good roads; church, post-office and lake within one mile of house; table liberally supplied with fresh vegetables, milk and good butter. References and full particulars on application.

JOHN E. CRANS—Farm-house. 3½ miles; accommodate 10; adults $5, children under ten years $3, transient $1; good fishing in the Stevensville Lake and Mongaup streams; all kinds of game; good livery; pleasant location; abundance of shade; veranda on south and east sides of house; pure water. References on application. Free transportation.

HARRISON DEWITT—DeWitt Cottage, boarding-house. 3 miles; accommodate 15; adults $5, children $3, transient $1; free transportation; raise our own vegetables; good fishing in Stevens Lake and the many trout streams in the vicinity; house is on the main street in the centre of the village; pleasantly located with plenty of shade; two minutes' walk to telegraph and post-office; spring-beds and excellent table.

Mrs. S. H. STEVENS—Farm-house. 3 miles; adults $6, children $3; free transportation; pleasant rooms and good country board; full particulars on application. Refers to E. C. Brinkman, No. 9 Third Place, Brooklyn; Fred Rogers, 272 Garden Street, Hoboken, N. J.

S. J. GREGORY—Gregory House. 3 miles; accommodate 20; adults $5 to $7; free transportation from station; located in village of Stevensville, which is on Liberty and White Lake turnpike; pleasantly situated on high ground; views of Walnut Mountain and surrounding country; good table; excellent water; daily mail; large and shaded grounds; convenient to church, telegraph and post-office; three minutes' walk from lake; livery. References on application.

CAMP LIFE ALONG THE BEAVERKILL.

W<small>M</small>. D<small>U</small>B<small>OIS</small>—Farm-house. 3 miles; accommodate 20; adults $5 to $7, children $2.50 to $3.50, transient $1; discount to season guests; oldest-established farm-house in the business; good fishing; first-class livery attached; well shaded; croquet and tennis grounds; free transportation. Refers to T. E. Greacen, 36 Warren Street, New York; Geo. Weir, 40 Warren Street, New York.

J. S. W<small>HEELER</small>—Farm-house. 3½ miles; accommodate 12; adults $6, children under ten $3, transient $1; plenty of shade; no malaria or mosquitoes; front porch 46 feet long; raise own vegetables; first-class livery attached; good gunning; free transportation for those staying two weeks or more. Refers to J. J. Adgate, 1260 Broadway, New York; D. C. Tallman, 104 W. 103d Street, New York.

W<small>ILLIS</small> S<small>LEATH</small>—Farm-house. 4½ miles; accommodate 15; adults $5 to $6.

LIBERTY, S<small>ULLIVAN</small> C<small>O</small>.

One of the most popular summer resorts in this section, situated 1,578 feet above tide-water, still in the valley of the middle Mongaup, a stream whose name signifies in Indian "dancing feather," and around which the glistening steel of the railway track winds in almost a true line of beauty, on its upward climb, two miles beyond, to the summit between the blue lake, Indian named Ontario, and the sea. To the north of the village lies a range of hills, more than 2,000 feet high, dappled with fields and woods, where the cosy farm-house nestles, and up whose sides the gardens climb. Westward lies Walnut Mountain, from whose summit eleven lakes, gleaming like silver shields in an emerald setting, may be seen with the naked eye. From this coign of vantage the vision may range from the wood-capped peaks of Pennsylvania to the crags of the Catskills, where the ghostly crew of Navigator Hudson keep their vigils, and where Rip Van Winkle took his nap.

[sidebar: 119 MILES FROM NEW YORK. FARE, $2.91; EXCURSION, $6.21.]

The whole panorama is "woodsey and wild and lonesome," east and west and north and south, while

"Along its tawny gravel-bed
Broad-flowing swift and still,
As if its meadows levels felt
The hurry of the hills "—

stretches the Mongaup.

"Noiseless between its banks of green
From curve to curve it slips;
The drowsy maple shadows rest
Like fingers on its lips."

The high altitude, with its cool, health-imparting breezes, combine to make Liberty very desirable as a summer home. The walks and drives about the country are beautiful and romantic. For all those who desire to pass a vacation amid beautiful scenery, pure air

VIEW OF THE NEVERSINK VALLEY FROM LIBERTY.

and water, with fresh and bountiful dairy products, amid streams and ponds well stocked with trout and bass, upland and marsh with whirring partridge and silent woodcock, we would suggest their locating in one of the quiet farm-houses mentioned in the following pages.

HOTEL WAWONDA.

(Cut on accompanying page.)

The finest-located and best-equipped house in Sullivan County. Elevation 2,000 feet; one mile from Liberty Station; main building 180 feet, with extension of 135 feet, and 650 feet of broad veranda, besides private balconies.

The house contains one hundred and fifty sleeping-rooms, large offices, parlors, etc., and the dining-room, parlors and main hall are heated by large open fireplaces; halls and offices heated by furnace; sleeping-rooms large, light and airy, with closets, presses, etc., high ceilings and perfect ventilation. The house is supplied with pure spring water from an adjacent mountain, and has baths, electric bells, and gas. Each floor is fitted with fire-hose, and electric fire-alarms. Everything to provide for the safety and comfort of the guests has been done, and the sanitary arrangements are perfect. The grounds comprise about fifty acres of field and wood. A short distance from the hotel on the grounds is a fine grove, nicely laid out with walks and seats. Bowling-alley and billiard-hall on the grounds for the exclusive use of the guests, also telegraph-office in the house.

There is not an objectionable room in the building, and the location is such that from all the many windows a magnificent view is obtainable, the scenery changing like a panorama. Looking southerly from the balconies, and the eye falls on the village of Liberty with its neat cottages embowered in shade; while to the eastward the peaks and crags of the Catskills and the Shawangunks arise to view. North and west the vision takes in the rounded summits of Walnut and Bald Top Mountains, with their farms and fields and lowing herds.

In the valley within one-half mile flows the crystal Mongaup, noted for its speckled beauties, while Stevensville, Revonah, Lilly and White lakes are only short drives distant. The site of this new summer home was selected from many in the vicinity as being " the chiefest among ten thousand and the one altogether lovely;" the elevation is high, and the ground slopes in every direction, giving perfect drainage.

The writer of the History of Sullivan County, speaking of the hills at and near this point, says that in sultry weather, when Æolus

HOTEL WAWONDA, LIBERTY, N. Y.—U. S. MESSITER, PROPRIETOR.

is elsewhere, still the refreshing breezes and gentle zephyrs are here toying with the daisies and coquetting with the leaves and clover. This has given birth to a tradition that the wind does not touch *terra firma*, from the time it leaves Lake Erie, until it reaches this "heaven-kissing hill."

The manager of the house is U. S. Messiter, a man well and favorably known to Liberty's summer visitors, and who, with his good wife, has been a popular caterer to their wants for years. The house will be run on temperance principles, and no liquors will be sold on the premises. The aim of the proprietors and manager is to furnish a first-class, ideal home for their guests, and they solicit the patronage of families who want a quiet resort with all home comforts, in which to enjoy their summer outing. No pains will be spared to make the stay of all who may be received pleasant and healthful. Large stables with good livery at reasonable rates. Carriages will meet guests at station on notification, and on arrival of all trains.

LIBERTY STATION—Liberty Post-Office.

HOTEL WAWONDA—1 mile from Liberty depot; accommodate 300; 150 sleeping-rooms, all large and airy; 650 feet of broad verandas; private balconies; description of house and grounds on preceding page. For circulars giving rates, address U. S. Messiter, Manager, Liberty, N. Y. Refers to J. E. Knox, care of Teft, Weller & Co., 328 Broadway, New York; R. G. Vassar, 51 W. 25th Street, New York; Rev. J. W. A. Dodge, Pastor of Chelsea M. E. Church, 30th Street, New York; G. H. Hallock, Jr., 401 Grand Street, New York; H. B. Bayles, M.D., 492 Ninth Street, Brooklyn, N. Y.; W. H. McCullam, M.D., 2 Lefferts Place, Brooklyn, N. Y.; Rev. J. M. Meeker, Pastor of Roseville M. E. Church, Newark, N. J.; Calvert Crary, 107 South Street, Boston, Mass.

Walnut Mountain Hotel

WALNUT MOUNTAIN HOTEL.

Walnut Mountain Hotel is situated one mile southwest of Liberty Village and railroad station. Private conveyance (upon notification) will meet guests. A drive of twenty minutes over a smooth, winding roadway brings you to the Mountain House and summit, 2,420 feet above sea-level.

The house is of modern design, special effort having been made to render it attractive and in harmony with its beautiful natural sur-

SKETCHES ABOUT WALNUT MOUNTAIN HOTEL.

roundings. It has all the conveniences of a first-class hotel, with accommodations for 120 guests. The halls and stairs are broad; open fireplaces; hot and cold water, etc.

Its elevation is such that the air is always cool and bracing. During the most heated portion of the summer the thermometer seldom rises above eighty-four degrees. Extensive and magnificent views are to be had in every direction.

For circulars giving terms, etc., address the manager, G. B. Holmes, Liberty, N. Y.

GILDERSLEVE HOUSE.

LIBERTY STATION—Liberty Post-Office.

GILDERSLEVE HOUSE, formerly the Willey House. This noted summer resort, owned by Richard Gildersleve, Clerk of Sullivan County, will again be conducted by him during the coming season. Terms $8 to $12; free transportation; elevation 2,000 feet; farm connected with the house; plenty of shade; fine walks and drives; croquet and tennis grounds; pure spring water in the house; milk and vegetables for table produced on farm; five minutes' walk from post-office and churches; in the vicinity of good hunting and fishing; no malaria. Refers to W. J. Martin, 56 Beaver Street, New York; W. H. Allen, Erie Dispatch, 401 Broadway, New York; Francis H. Ludlow, Drexel Building, corner Wall and Broad Streets, New York; J. L. Remond, Nassau and Washington Streets, Brooklyn, N. Y.; Dr. J. W. Richardson, 76 Washington Place, New York; James McCullough, 352 Fulton Street, Brooklyn, N. Y.

G. W. MURPHY, Manager—Mansion House, formerly known as the Clements House, owned by John Murphy, will be conducted by himself and son; accommodate 80; adults $7 to $10, transient $1.50. House has been entirely renovated, both inside and out, making extensive lawns for tennis, croquet and base-ball games. Being centrally located, it is one of the finest hotels in Liberty; free transportation to and from all trains; table and appointments unexcelled; air pure and dry; malaria and mosquitoes unknown; balconies on the second and third floors; bath-rooms and all sanitary improvements; pure spring water from the mountains; parties visiting Liberty and vicinity prospecting will find agreeable accommodations at the Mansion House, where the finest livery can be secured at a nominal price; good hunting and fishing. Correspondence will receive prompt attention. Refers to W. Watkins, 16 Catharine Street, New York; J. Cherry, 336 W. 145th Street, New York; John Loughlin, 27 Atlantic Avenue, Brooklyn, N. Y.; George Randall, 104 Reid Avenue, Brooklyn, N. Y.; H. F. Beakey, 295 Hoyt Street, Brooklyn, N. Y.

D. C. FRANCISCO—Liberty Springs House, boarding and farm-house. 1 mile; accommodates 40; rates, adults $8 to $9, children $5, transient $1.50; discount to season guests; free transportation; 250 feet of veranda; fine scenery; high elevation; sanitary arrangements perfect; hot and cold water, bath, croquet, lawn tennis, swings, etc.; five minutes' walk from the largest boarding-house in Sullivan County. Refers to E. P. Walker, Cotton Exchange, New York; Mrs. N. E. Thill, 611 Wythe Avenue, Brooklyn; Mrs. J. O'Brien, 460 W. 43d Street, New York; Miss M. T. Murphy, 314 E. 84th Street, New York.

LAWRENCE MCGRATH—Hotel. Five minutes' walk from depot; adults $7, no children taken, transient $1; discount to season guests; raise own vegetables; first-class livery; convenient to churches; 4 miles from White Sulphur Springs; good roads; excellent gunning and fishing; first-class table; delightful scenery; pure water; very healthy. Full particulars furnished on application.

H. KEEGAN—Farm-house. 1 mile; accommodate 20; adults $6 to $7, children $4 and $5, transient $1.25; free transportation; raise our own vegetables; good fishing in Stevensville, Mongaup and Broadhead lakes; good livery accommodations; house stands on elevated ground, surrounded with fruit and shade trees; free from malaria; have large play-grounds; first-class table, with abundance of fresh milk, butter, eggs, chickens and vegetables. Tally-ho stages for White Lake pass the door. References on application.

D. R. BONNELL—Farm-house. 2½ miles; accommodate 35; adults $5 to $7, children $3 to 4; free transportation; house is new, and surroundings are pleasant; raise our own vegetables; excellent fishing and gunning; first-class livery; ample shade; pure water; liberal table; rooms large and airy; large piazza; piano; abundance of fruit; no Hebrews wanted; have enlarged my house and made general improvements. Refers to Mr. O. Schwerdtfeger, 887 Lafayette Avenue, Brooklyn, N. Y.; William S. Weasley, 47 Cedar Street, New York.

E. E. PINNEY—Pinney House. Situated one mile east of Liberty; accommodate 60 to 70; house and furniture new; large and airy rooms; first-class beds; a shady piazza 80 feet long; plenty of shade trees; trout stream running through farm; splendid view of Catskill, Shawangunk and Walnut Mountains; ten minutes' drive to depot and church; good livery in connection; free transportation; raise own vegetables. References on application.

J. N. HARDENBURGH—Farm boarding-house. 1 mile; accommodate 30; adults $6 to $7, children under eight half price, transient $1.50; discount to season guests; free transportation; we have a farm of 70 acres situated on the south side of Surnac Point; ½ mile from and overlooking the village of Liberty and surrounding country for many miles; we keep horses, cows, chickens, and furnish our own milk and eggs, maple sugar and honey; there is a small trout stream running through the farm; excellent gunning and fishing; ½ mile from church. Refers to Mrs. C. F. Napier, 1423 Pacific Street, Brooklyn, N. Y.

GEORGE B. HOLMES—Walnut Mountain House. Opens June 9th, for its sixth season; patronized only by the most refined class, and a place where rest, quietness and comforts of home life are obtained at a moderate price, but enough to guarantee first-class service in every way. Circulars, terms, description of rooms, etc., on application.

ABEL GREGORY—Lake Farm Boarding-house. 3½ miles; accommodate 30; 18 rooms; terms on application; free transportation for season guests; plenty of shade; good water; no malaria; lake near house; boats and piano for use of guests; daily mail; good fishing; plenty of eggs, milk and butter; good livery; house open from June 1st to November 1st. References on application.

GEORGE CRARY—Farm-house. 1½ miles; accommodate 25; terms on application; discount to season guests; free transportation; excellent fishing and gunning; good livery; raise own vegetables; 1½ miles to church; excellent table; house has been enlarged and improved, and will be enabled to accommodate guests better than ever before. Refers to John H Parsons, 132 Nassau Street, New York.

C. M. BONNELL—Private cottage. ½ mile; accommodate 15 to 20; adults $7 to 10; house is newly built and furnished with all modern improvements; rooms are large and airy and nicely furnished; pure spring water; excellent table; high and healthy location which commands a fine view of the village and surrounding country. Refers to W. J. Martin, 56 Beaver Street, New York, and Elton Clark, Hanover Bank or 158 West 120th Street, New York.

Mrs. W. BRODHEAD—Proprietor of Rose Cottage, ½ mile; accommodate 20 to 25; adults $5, $6 and $7 per week, children $3 to $5, transient according to rooms; discount for families for season; free transportation; discount in September and October; ¼ mile from church; house nicely located; ample shade; large and airy rooms; plenty of milk and eggs; pure spring water; raise own vegetables; first-class fishing; good table. References on application.

R. R. SHERWOOD—Farm-house. 2½ miles; accommodate 6; adults $6, children $4; free transportation; fine farm of 250 acres near Walnut Mountain and Stevensville Lake; plenty of milk, butter and eggs; running spring water; good fishing and gunning. Gentlemen or families without children preferred.

Residence of J. H. Allen.

J. C. Hall, Proprietor.

Du Nord House—J. H. Duhrmann, Proprietor.

White Sulphur Springs House—Henry Ernhout, Proprietor.

Residence of D. Polleyman.

Nichols & Son, Proprietors.

PROMINENT HOUSES AT LIBERTY.

JOHN REDINGTON—Farm-house. ¼ mile; accommodate 25; rates on application; discount to season guests; free transportation; large, airy rooms; house situated on high ground, the farm contains 200 acres, commanding a view of the surrounding country; plenty of shade; pleasant walks and drives; excellent table; large piazza; piano; livery attached. References exchanged; correspondence solicited.

HENRY INTEMANN—Helena House. 2 miles; accommodate 20; terms $5 to $7; free transportation; located on high ground, near Walnut Mountain; abundance of shade; pure running spring water. References on application.

Mrs. EDWIN FORBES—Woodbine Cottage.- ¼ mile; accommodate 20; terms $7 to $8; pleasantly situated on high ground; large, airy rooms; good sanitary arrangements; pure water; adults wishing a quiet home preferred. References on application.

Mrs. H. A. DARBEE—Private boarding-house. ¼ mile; accommodate 20; adults $7 to $10, transient $1.50; raise our own vegetables; good fishing and gunning; first-class livery; three minutes' walk from church; liberal table. References exchanged.

E. S. PIERSON—Farm-house. ¼ mile; accommodate 12; adults $6 to $7; discount to season guests; house pleasantly located; plenty of shade; beautiful scenery; charming walks and drives; first-class livery; excellent table; large and comfortable rooms, nicely furnished; pure water; home comforts; bracing air. References and full particulars on application.

L. B. GORTON—Overlook House. ¼ mile; accommodate 30; adults $6 to $8; house overlooks village; mountain scenery; shade; natural woods; no dust; cool, quiet, large rooms; good table; piano; home comforts; ten minutes' walk to post-office and churches.

Mrs. C. L. CARRIER—Carrier Cottage. ½ mile; accommodate 12; adults $6 to $7, transient $1.25; eight large, airy rooms, well supplied with closets; house well located; five minutes' walk to church; good gunning and fishing; first-class livery; excellent table. Refers to Rev. Thos. M. Webb, Liberty, N. Y.

W. M. ROOSA—Shady Grove Farm. 1½ miles; accommodate 30; adults $5 to $7, children $2 to $5, transient $1; raise own vegetables; good fishing and hunting; free transportation; good livery; large orchard; plenty of fruit. Refers to F. Duncomb, 214 East Broadway, New York; O. C. Henry, 105 Monroe Street, New York.

D. BRUCE SCHOONMAKER—Farm-house. 3 miles; free transportation; accommodate 20; terms on application; discount for season guests; good hunting and fishing; raise own vegetables; occasional free rides to church, three miles distant; excellent table. Write for particulars.

JOHN BENGEL—Grand View Farm House. 2 miles; accommodate 25; adults $5 to $6, children $3, transient $1.25; free transportation; house located on top of mountain; 2,000 feet elevation; double piazza; plenty of shade; magnificent views in every direction; maple grove adjacent to house; table supplied with best of farm products, such as milk, eggs, maple syrup and vegetables; good fishing and hunting. Refers to E. F. Leber, 5 William Street, New York; C. G. Kroll, 315 W. 27th Street, New York; C. B. Schaidner, 183 E. 124th Street, New York.

J. C. HALL—The Hall House. ¼ mile; accommodate 50; transportation free; a fine new building, large and spacious; finely located immediately in the village of Liberty, overlooking the main part of the town, 1,600 feet elevation; 24 large and airy bedrooms, consisting of suites of rooms, adjoining rooms, and two lovely bay-window rooms; inspection solicited; house open all the year; season guests desired and adults preferred; no reduction for children; rates $2 per day; special rates for the season; no Hebrews taken. References: Wm. G. DeWitt, 88 Nassau Street, New York; H. B. Bayles, M.D., 442 Ninth Street, Brooklyn, N. Y.

JOHN H. ALLEN—Boarding-house. Accommodate 25; adults $7 to $10, children $5, transient $1.50; discount to season guests; raise our own vegetables; house situated on Chestnut Street, at an elevation commanding a splendid view of the surrounding country; lot contains 4 acres; spring water; lawn tennis; fresh milk and eggs. Refers to Thos. P. Goodrich, 409 Broadway, New York; F. F. Grant, 309 Vanderbilt Avenue, Brooklyn, and Mrs. Briggs, or Mrs. James, 1328 Pacific Street, Brooklyn.

J. A. CLEMENTS—Farm-house. 1½ miles; accommodate 20; terms on application; guests met at train free of charge; private pond with boats, no charge; raise our own vegetables; beautifully located and well shaded.

Liberty House.

Residence of C. M. Bonnett.

Residence of J. R. Carver.

Residence of J. D. Scott.

G. R. Carver, Proprietor.

Mansion House.

PROMINENT HOUSES AT LIBERTY.

M. Schaefer—Hotel. At Station; accommodate 15; 12 rooms; transient $1; fine rooms; pleasant walks; delightful, invigorating air; free from malaria; ample shade; house furnished with home comforts; good table. Refers to H. S. Heydon, 44 Harrison Avenue, Brooklyn, N. Y.

J. B. Nichols & Son—Maple View House. 1 mile; accommodate 70; adults $7 to $12; the house is situated on an eminence which commands a grand view, surrounded by large, amply shaded lawns; tennis courts, croquet grounds, etc.; is connected with a productive farm, enabling the proprietors to furnish everything pure and fresh; house has been recently enlarged and refurnished, so that it is attractive and pleasant; large piazzas and private balconies surround the house; rooms large and airy and provided with closets; piano; spring water; perfect sanitary arrangements; livery and boarding stables; no Jews wanted, and not many children. It is the proprietors' desire to make this place first-class in every particular; inspection solicited. Circulars, references, etc., on application.

Henry Ishutz—Farm-house. Thirty minutes' drive from depot; accommodate 20; adults $6 to $7, children $5, transient $1.50; free transportation; raise own vegetables; good table; excellent water; romantic walks and drives. Correspondence solicited. References on application.

A. H. Coleman, Liberty—Maple Grove Boarding-house. 1 mile; accommodate 20; terms on application; transient $1; good gunning and fishing in Mongaup pond near the house; religious people preferred; 1 mile from church; free transportation to and from station. Reference: Rev. Geo. T. Beswick, 123 South 3d Street, Brooklyn, N. Y.

Mrs. George Cooper—Farm-house. Short distance from depot; accommodate 30; adults $6 to $7, children under ten years half rates; plenty of shade; fresh eggs, milk and vegetables right from the farm. References and full particulars on application.

Mrs. Erastus Young—Private boarding-house. Near station; accommodate 20; pleasant views; fine rooms; fresh eggs, cream, vegetables and all varieties of a well-ordered table. Correspondence solicited. Terms and full particulars on application.

C. J. Fohrman—Grandeur View House. ¼ mile; accommodate 30; rates on application; pure spring water; high and healthy location; raise our own vegetables; good table; plenty of milk, eggs and farm products. References on application.

Phebe Low, M. D.—Physician's Residence. ¾ mile; accommodate 15; adults $5 to $8; raise our own vegetables; light, airy rooms; good running water; convenient to post-office, churches and station; attractive grounds; plenty of shade. Refers to Dr. J. L. Lynch, 358 W. 36th Street, New York.

E. R. Morton—Farm-house. Accommodate 5; adults $6, children $3, transient $1; pleasant surroundings; good table; pure water; raise own vegetables; home comforts; pleasant walks and drives. Full particulars and references on application.

H. T. Lewis—Farm-house. 2 miles; ten minutes' walk from Revonah Lake; rates and references on application; good table; pleasant surroundings; romantic walks and drives. Refers to Edw'd Lafage, 262 Tompkins Avenue, Brooklyn, N. Y.

J. M. Hill—Private cottage. ¼ mile; accommodate 20; adults $7 to $10; high and healthy location; nice lawn; pure spring water; large and nicely furnished rooms; first-class livery; good fishing; near church; free transportation; no Jews wanted. Refers to T. P. Goodrich, 409 Broadway, New York; W. A. Gedney, 42 W. 67th Street, New York.

Thomas H. Houlihan—Liberty House. ¼ mile; accommodate 60; 40 rooms; adults $7 to $10, transient $1.50 per day; discount to season boarders; free transportation to and from all trains; centrally located; large, airy rooms; fine tennis and croquet grounds; abundance of shade; table furnished with the best in the market; first-class livery connected with the house; raise our own vegetables; good fishing and gunning; no pains spared for the comfort of guests; parties visiting Liberty and vicinity prospecting for board will find agreeable accommodations at the Liberty House, and livery will be furnished with competent and well-informed drivers to convey prospectors around the country; charges reasonable. Refers to C. Patterson & Son, 71 Wall Street, New York; Charles Jewett, M. D., 307 Gates Avenue, Brooklyn, N. Y.; L. S. Schermerhorn, 2 West 83d Street, N. Y.; Mark Curley, Jersey City Supply Co., 89 Railroad Avenue, Jersey City, N. J.

E. W. Schubert—Hotel. Near station; pleasantly situated; large, airy rooms; comfortable beds; pure spring water; good table; daily mail; pleasant walks and drives; good livery; convenient to church. Full particulars on application.

WILLIAM DWYER—Cold Spring Cottage. 1 mile; accommodate 16; adults $6; free transportation; house surrounded by fruit and shade trees; large and beautiful lawns; table abundantly supplied with pure milk, fresh eggs, butter and poultry; pure spring water; good fishing and hunting; raise our own vegetables. Refers to R. S. Treacy, 265 West 42d Street, New York, and Mrs. J. O'Brien, 460 West 43d Street, New York.

CLARK KRUM—Brookdale Farm House. 3½ miles; accommodate 20; adults $6, children $4, transient $1; free transportation; situated on high ground; good water; good roads; plenty of shade; raise our own vegetables; good pickerel and trout fishing in Stevensville Lake; good gunning—partridge, rabbit, woodcock, etc.; three miles from church. References on application.

ELIHU HULL—Farm-house. ½ mile; accommodate 35; adults $6 to $7; house newly built and pleasantly located; large rooms, well furnished; pure spring water; plenty of shade; free transportation. References on application.

FRED DOHRMANN—Chestnut Ridge House. 2 miles; accommodate 75; adults $6, children $4, good fishing and gunning; all kinds of game; vegetables served from our own farm; pleasant surroundings; home comforts; bountiful table; pure spring water. References on application.

Mrs. AMANDA SHAW—Fernwood Cottage Farm House. 1½ miles; accommodate 15; adults $6, children $4, transient $1; situated on the Blue Mountains, overlooking the village; one of the finest views in the county can be obtained here, the Catskills and Shawangunk Mountains are plainly visible; first-class livery; boating and fishing. Correspondence solicited.

"CARRIER GRAND VIEW," J. B. Carrier, proprietor—¼ mile; accommodate 50; adults $8 to $12; special rate for families; discount to season guests, also for the months of May, June and October; pleasant rooms; lawn tennis and croquet grounds; livery attached; accommodation for those wishing to bring their own horses and carriages; cottage to let in village for summer season. As its name implies, the Grand View has a location affording pleasant views in every direction, overlooks the village of Liberty, and commands extensive views of the Shawangunk and Catskill Mountains; the mountain air always circulating makes it cool and healthy. Refers to Floyd Vail, 52 Broadway, New York; Fred W. Krugler, Times Building, Room 25, New York; Frederick M. Evarts, 62 Wall Street, New York; Judge Garrick, 19 Duncan Avenue, Jersey City Heights, N. J., and Mrs. R. B. Malone, 213 South 9th Street, Brooklyn, N. Y.

Mrs. J. H. VAN ORDEN—Pleasant View House (fourth season). ¼ mile; accommodate 20; adults $5 to $8, transient $1; house newly built on an elevation of 2,000 feet above tide-water, overlooking village; free from dust and noise of the street; natural woods close to house; 80 feet of shaded veranda; pure spring water; good table; ¼ mile from church. Refers to Capt. Michael Freel, 176 Skillman Street, Brooklyn, N. Y.; U. S. Messiter, Liberty, N. Y., and J. G. Case, 143 Liberty Street, Room 205, New York.

Mrs. DAVID CLEMENTS—Boarding-house. Five minutes' walk from depot; accommodate 20; rates on application; house is nicely located; well shaded with maples; large and comfortable rooms; raise our own vegetables; churches near by. Correspondence solicited.

Mrs. H. M. DEVINE—Sylvan Grove Cottages, to let furnished, also boarders accommodated. Farmhouse. ¾ mile from depot and post-office; well-shaded grounds; pure running spring water; stabling for horses. Full particulars on application.

"THE LODGE"—Ravonah Lake, will be opened June 1st, 1892. Accommodate 25; situation superior to any in Sullivan County; 2,500 feet above tide-water; near Ravonah Lake; fine drives and rambles in forest; beautiful view over the village and valleys; board $10 per week. Apply with references to Ravonah Park Lodge, Liberty, N. Y.

Mrs. H. ERNHOUT—Hill Side Vills. Accommodate 50; adults preferred; beautifully located; large and pleasant rooms, comfortably furnished; excellent table; pure spring water; ample shade; bracing mountain air; 2,500 feet above tide-water; romantic walks and drives; first-class livery; good roads; home comforts. Rates, references and full particulars on application.

JOHN H. DOHRMANN—Du Nord. Five minutes' walk from depot; accommodate 100; terms on application; transient $1.50; house is located on high ground, with beautiful views in all directions; good fishing and gunning; first-class livery; table well supplied with everything that is first-class; good rooms; beautiful scenery; charming walks and drives; pure water. Refers to Richard Helms, 101 Bank Street, New York; Jacob Hahn, 453 Third Avenue, New York, and H. Dunekack, 180 Dean Street, Brooklyn, N. Y.

JAMES SCHOONMAKER—Farm-house. 2½ miles; accommodate 30; adults $5 to $10, according to rooms and number in each room; free transportation to and from depot; fine views; large piazza with good shade; excellent drives; Mongaup stream passes through the farm; good livery at reasonable rates; raise our own vegetables; very desirable house. Refers to Mr. Thomas J. Meighan, 235 East 125th Street, and Mr. Chas. McCullough, 25 Perry Street, New York.

ALTON E. FULLER—Village residence. ½ mile; accommodate 12; house is new and newly fitted for summer boarders; on high ground; pleasant walks and drives; good, fresh air; raise our own vegetables; good gunning and fishing; fine livery; ¼ mile from church; excellent table; delightful surroundings; home comforts. References and full particulars furnished on application.

E. W. GRANT—Grant Cottage. ¼ mile; accommodate 20; adults $6 to $10; situated on sightly ground; rooms large and pleasant; house new and neatly furnished; raise our own vegetables; fresh eggs and milk; good table. Reference on application.

R. R. RAY—Farm-house. 1½ miles; accommodate 12; adults $6, children $4.

GEORGE HILL—Farm-house. 3½ miles; accommodate 25. Terms and particulars on application.

Mrs. EMILY C. MORTON—Accommodate 12; adults $5 to $6, children half rates.

WILLIAM F. SHERWOOD, M.D.—Accommodate 10; adults $7. Write for particulars.

JANE GREGORY—Farm-house. Pleasantly situated; good table; good fishing; livery attached. Particulars on application.

C. W. CALKINS—Accommodate 25; adults $6 to $8. Full particulars on application.

B. W. GREGORY—Gregory Homestead. Accommodate 24; adults preferred. Correspondence solicited.

EDWARD CHAMPLIN—Farm-house. ½ mile; accommodate 10. Correspondence solicited.

C. R. GREGORY—Will accommodate 40 guests in 1892.

Mrs. H. A. BRIDGES—Farm-house. 1 mile; accommodate 10. Terms and full particulars on application.

Mrs. MARY E. TEEPLE—Boarding-house. Adults $6 to $8, children $3 to $5.

Mrs. ANN CARRIER—Accommodate 30; adults $5 to $6, children $3.

Mrs. V. CHAMPLIN—Village residence. Accommodate 30. Terms on application.

GEORGE J. MORRIS—Farm-house. References and particulars on application. No children desired.

Mrs. B. W. WIMMER—Boarding-house. Accommodate 20. Terms and references on application.

FOR SALE.

AT LIBERTY, N. Y.—A modern new cottage of 12 rooms; 50 feet of piazza; fine view of the surrounding country; good drainage; 5 minutes from post-office and railroad depot; good garden; nice lawn; reasonable price. Address, Lock Box 2, Liberty, N. Y.

LIBERTY STATION—Neversink Post-Office.

H. W. DEAN—Neversink Valley House. 6 miles; accommodate 150; 60 rooms; adults $6 to $10, children $3 to $7, transient $1 to $2; discount to season guests; good boating near house; four cottages convenient; raise our own vegetables; good fishing in Neversink and other small streams—trout, pickerel, etc.; gunning for partridge, woodcock and rabbit, which are abundant; excellent livery; convenient to church; romantic and picturesque surroundings; bracing air; spring water in all parts of the house; large, shaded lawn; hall for dancing; first-class piano; telephone connecting with telegraph. References on application.

SCRIBNER BROS.—Accommodate 30; adults $7 to $10. Write for particulars.

E. VANDERLYN—Accommodate 30; adults $6, children $3. Write for particulars.

CALVIN D. HORNBECK—Accommodate 20; adults $6, transient $1. Write for particulars.

W. H. H. WILLIAMS—Maple Grove House. 5 miles; accommodate 200; adults $8 to $15, transient $1.50 to $2.50; special rates for May, June and October; transportation 50 cents, trunks 25 cents; a popular summer resort, located among the hills of Sullivan County, N. Y., 1,600 feet above tide-water; no malaria; pure water from mountain spring; bath-rooms with hot and cold water; pleasant drives and walks; daily mail; telephone in the house connecting with telegraph; house greatly improved; good fishing and gunning; ¼ mile from church; good livery. Refers to N. S. Westcott, M. D., 156 West 12th Street; D. G. Harriman, 19 Park Place; B. S. Waters, Bank of Metropolis, New York; and Dr. J. B. Brown, 80 Lafayette Avenue, Brooklyn, N. Y.

YOUNGSVILLE, SULLIVAN CO.,

Is eight miles west of Liberty, and reached by daily stage. It opens its doors each summer, and receives in its hotels and farm-houses many summer boarders. This is a splendid locality for trout-fishing and for the smaller game in its season.

LIBERTY STATION—Youngsville Post-Office.

MRS. L. P. MYERS—Hotel. Acommodate 30; adults $5 to $6, children half. Correspondence solicited.

EDWARD HOMER—Hotel and boarding-house. 8 miles; accommodate 40; adults $6, children under ten years half rate, transient $1; excellent trout and black-bass fishing; guides furnished at reasonable rates; livery connected with hotel; three churches within ¼ mile; raise own vegetables; free transportation to and from station; this hotel has every convenience for the comfort of guests; 1,800 feet above the sea; plenty of shade; splendid surroundings. Refers to Geo. Schenk, 93 Sixth Avenue, New York; P. Coffee, 354 Second Street, South Brooklyn, N. Y., and Robt. Oestricher, 30 Union Square, New York.

W. H. KAYS—Hunters' and Fishermen's House. 8 miles; accommodate 48; adults $6, children $2.50, transient $1; discount to season guests; Sand Pond and Stevensville Lake near by, which affords excellent trout, bass, pickerel and perch fishing; boats and fishing-tackle free to guests; raise own vegetables; charming surroundings. Refers to Thomas Vincent, Orange, N. J.; Harry Thompson, Newark, N. J.

LIBERTY STATION—Briscoe Post-Office.

W. H. STEPHENSON—Buena Vista Cottage. 7 miles; accommodate 25; adults $6, children $3 to $4, transient $1; discount to season guests; raise our own vegetables; good gunning; excellent fishing in Stevensville and Briscoe lakes; comfortable rooms; good table. References on application.

LIBERTY STATION—Stevensville Post-Office.

J. H. KILCOIN—Hotel. 3 miles; accommodate 25; adults $5 to $7, children half rates, transient $1.25; free transportation; near Stevensville Lake; house newly built; rooms large and airy; dancing once a week; discount to season guests; raise own vegetables; 100 feet piazza; good livery; five minutes' walk from church; good fishing. References on application.

MRS. WILLIAM LENNON—Farm-house. 3 miles; accommodate 20; adults $6 to $8, children half, transient $1.50; discount to season guests; free transportation; house beautifully situated; rooms large and airy; plenty of shade; pleasant views; daily mail; five minutes' walk to post-office; good pickerel-fishing in Stevensville Lake; plenty of fresh milk, eggs and poultry; raise our own vegetables; excellent gunning. References exchanged.

LIBERTY STATION—Jeffersonville Post-Office.

AUGUSTUS GROUTEN—Boarding-house. 12 miles; accommodate 15; adults $5 to $6, children $3 to $4, transient $1.

CHARLES HOMER—New Hotel. 12 miles; accommodate 40; adults $6 to $7, children half price, transient $1.

CHARLES W. WILFERT—Farm-house. 10 miles; accommodate 15; adults $6, children $3, transient $1.

JOHN S. DIEHL—Boarding-house. 12 miles; accommodate 30; adults $7, children half, transient $1.

W. H. H. WILLIAMS HOUSE NEVERSINK.

WHITE SULPHUR SPRINGS

Are situated four miles from Liberty, the drive from the latter point being most beautiful and attractive. The analysis of the water as made by Dr. Tomlinson, of New York, is given herewith. It is used with the most gratifying results for all kidney-diseases, dyspepsia and impure blood, and will cure all skin-diseases and nervous debility, loss of appetite and torpid liver; also will give great relief in all cases of rheumatism, dropsy, scrofula and chronic diseases. Mr. Henry Ernhout opened last season a new summer house, accommodating about 150 guests; with ample grounds and lawns, hot and cold sulphur baths, etc.

ANALYSIS:

Chloride of Sodium.
Chloride of Potassium.
Bicarbonate of Soda.
Bicarbonate of Ammonia.
Bicarbonate of Magnesia.
Bicarbonate of Iron.
Nitrate of Potassa.

Alumina.
Sulphate of Soda.
Sulphate of Magnesia.
Sulphate of Potassa.
Carbonate of Lithia.
Organic matters.
Carbonate of Acid Gas.

LIBERTY STATION—White Sulphur Springs Post-Office.

EBEN HILL—Farm-house. 4 miles; free transportation; accommodate 30; adults $5 to $8, children half rates; raise own vegetables; good fishing; first-class livery; short distance from church, post and telegraph offices; house located on high and dry ground, with double piazza, from which are some of the grandest views in the country; elevation 1,800 feet; bracing air; good water, with the benefits to be derived from the White Sulphur Springs, make this a very desirable place, especially for invalids. Refers to C. R. Badeau, 131 Halsey Street, Brooklyn; E. A. Geo. Pritemann, 53 Sixth Avenue, New York.

JONATHAN L. LAWRENCE—Farm-house. 5 miles; accommodate 16; adults $6, children under twelve $3; discount to season guests; raise our own vegetables; good fishing and gunning; ½ mile from church and post-office; good table; charming surroundings; home comforts; bracing air. Refers to Lewis Robie, 169 Eighth Avenue, New York; J. Adams, Broadway and 19th Street, New York.

HENRY ERNHOUT—Hotel. 4 miles; accommodate 125; adults $7 to $15, children $5 to $8, transient $2; situated at the upper portion of the ravine, has been constructed a beautiful lake, well stocked with trout, and furnished with boats for the accommodation of guests at a nominal charge; special rates for May, June and October; excellent gunning; first-class livery attached; raise own vegetables; transportation from depot 50 cents, trunks 25 cents; 60 large and comfortable sleeping-rooms; within five minutes' walk of church. First-class references and full particulars on application.

PERRY DE WITT—Farm-house. 5 miles: accommodate 8; adults $6 to $7, children $3 to $4, transient $1.25; free transportation: delightfully situated on high ground; plenty of shade; pure air; spring water; free from mosquitoes and malaria; plenty of fresh eggs, milk and butter; raise our own vegetables; good fishing; own livery; near church. Refers to Wm. Swan, 668 First Avenue, New York, and H. A. Meyer, 252 Wythe Avenue, Brooklyn, N. Y.

JOHN WILLIE—Farm-house. 5 miles; accommodate 10; adults $6 to $7, children $3 to $4, transient $1.25; on notice will meet guests at depot, and transport them free; house delightfully situated on high ground, with large piazza; plenty of shade; bracing air; no mosquitoes; near four churches, and a short distance from White Sulphur Springs; plenty of fresh eggs, milk, and butter; raise our own vegetables; excellent fishing and gunning; our own livery. For references and full information apply to the above address.

WHITE SULPHUR SPRINGS.

M. E. HALL—Farm-house. 5 miles; accommodate 20; terms on application; good fishing and gunning; small brook running through farm; plenty of shade; good table; delightful surroundings; romantic walks and drives; finest scenery; bracing air; pure water; home comforts; raise our own vegetables; ½ mile from church, and ¼ mile from Sulphur Springs. Refers to G. M. Hughes, 381 Broadway, New York; J. Butterworth, 159 Front Street, New York, and U. S. Messiter, Liberty, N. Y.

H. S. WOOD—Farm-house. 5 miles; accommodate 25; adults $5 to $8, children $3 to $5, transient $1; discount to season guests; good fishing and gunning; livery attached; short distance from church; daily mail; telegraph office short distance from house; transportation free. References on application.

JOHN D. LEWIS—Boarding-house. Accommodate 12; adults $5 to $7. Particulars on application.

WHITE LAKE, SULLIVAN CO.

For half a century this spot has been a favorite resort for sportsmen, invalids and pleasure-seekers. During the winter of 1885–86 the Liberty and White Lake Turnpike was organized, and a magnificent road built between these points, on which a line of tally-ho coaches run, connecting with all trains. The route was very largely patronized, and became at once the popular route to this resort. The drive from Liberty to White Lake is one of great beauty and interest. The scenery of Sullivan County is noted, but this lake, with its surroundings, is unsurpassed for beauty and attractive loveliness. It is the largest of a group of sixteen lakes in the centre of the town of Bethel, and receives its name from the whiteness of the sand on its shore and bottom, and the beautiful transparency of its waters. Its Indian name, Lake Kauneonga, is much prettier and more appropriate. It is elevated some 1,500 feet above the sea, and is consequently free from from malaria influences, with an atmosphere uniformly cool during the summer months.

LIBERTY STATION—White Lake Post-Office.

JOHN J. VAN ORDEN—West Shore House. Accommodate 40; adults $7 to $8, transient $1.50; house located on shore of lake, lately enlarged and newly fitted up; new piano; large, airy rooms, commanding the finest views of the lake; abundance of shade; piazza around the house; boats to let at reasonable rates; livery connected with the house; new carriage-house for parties desiring to bring horses; raise our own vegetables, and have the same cook as last season; fine croquet and tennis court. Refers to M. C. Norton, 108 Huron Street, Brooklyn; E. Recker, 151 Van Buren Street, Brooklyn; Frank McLaughlin, 156 Roebling Street, Brooklyn; R. J. Darlington, 481 Bedford Avenue, Brooklyn; W. H. Botsford, 68 Wall Street, New York; Chas. Putnam, 347 W. 19th Street, New York; Frederick B. Warde, 27 Halsey Street, Brooklyn, N. Y.; E. F. Greene, 260 Lenox Avenue, New York.

J. F. CALLBREATH—Lakeside House. Accommodate 80; terms for June $7, July and August $8 to $10; house has been enlarged, and is pleasantly located on the borders of the lake, 1,800 feet above the tide; 250 feet of piazza; shade trees; lawn tennis, croquet; stables and boats; good fishing and gunning; milk, eggs and vegetables from our own farm; no malaria; no mosquitoes; no whiskey; daily mail, telegraph and tally-ho; cold spring water on the premises. References on application.

J. E. GRAY—White Lake Spring House. 9 miles; accommodate 50; adults $7 to $10, children's rates on application, transient $2; good table, plentifully supplied with fresh vegetables, milk, eggs and chickens; cuisine will be under the same management as last season; halls and public rooms large and airy; recent improvements made on house and grounds; fine piano; good boats at reasonable rates; good fishing and gunning; first-class livery; five minutes' walk to church; horses boarded. References: James A. Harper, 4 Irving Place, New York; D. G. Hollis, 110 Fort Green Place, Brooklyn; A. W. Guilbert, 1266 Broadway, New York.

J. E. GRAY SPRING HOUSE.   SHERMAN RAMSAY HOUSE.

SHERMAN RAMSAY—Ramsay House. 9 miles; accommodate 30; pleasantly situated; no mosquitoes; good table; pure water; ice always on hand; vegetables from our own garden; excellent fishing—bass and pickerel; boats to let at reasonable rates; stages pass the door; transportation from Liberty, $1; good livery. Terms, references and further information given on application.

P. HUFF—White Lake House. Accommodate 48; terms on application. This house commands the finest position of any at the lake, the situation being on an eminence near the southeastern end of this beautiful sheet of water, and overlooks a large portion of Sullivan, Ulster and Greene counties, with their fine mountain ranges; broad piazza; rooms all large and airy; broad halls; wide and easy stairway; fine piano; dancing and other amusements, and a good time guaranteed; croquet grounds; lawn tennis; nice walks and drives; ample accommodations for horses and carriages; boats on premises. Open year round.

PAUL VON MORSTEIN—The Von Morstein Villa. 9 miles; accommodate 20; adults $7, special rates for children, transient $1; discount to season guests; excellent fishing; raise own vegetables; game, partridges and rabbits; ½ mile to church; German and English spoken; comfortable rooms; clean beds; piano, tennis, croquet, hammocks, boating, driving, etc.; persons desiring a quiet, comfortable home should communicate with owner. Refers to J. M. Hartt, 325 Marcy Avenue, Brooklyn; Mrs. S. Bloch, 367 Union Street, Brooklyn, N. Y.

D. B. KINNE—White Lake Mansion House. 9 miles; accommodate 100; adults $8 to $12, transient $2; a first-class hotel, furnished in good style, and well adapted for the comfort of summer boarders; located near the shore of lake; noted for purity of air and beauty of scenery; two cottages connected with house; good bass, pickerel and trout fishing; send for circular. References on application.

W. C. KINNE—Prospect House. Accommodate 75; 40 rooms; rates as low as consistent with satisfactory accommodations and table; situated on high ground overlooking the lake, and commands an extensive view of fields and forests, hills and mountains; rooms thoroughly ventilated and well furnished; halls and public rooms large and airy; 150-foot piazza; abundant supply of pure water; grove well supplied with seats on lake-shore; tennis court; a lot of new cedar boats, which will be kept in good order, will be let at reasonable rates by the day or week.

TROUT-FISHING ON THE WILLOWEMOC.

CHALON LEWIS—"Lewis Cottage," farm-house. 9 miles; accommodate 10; adults $6; discount to season guests; ten minutes' walk from church and post-office; plenty of shade; raise own vegetables; pleasant and healthy location; excellent table; pure water. References and circulars on application.

THOMAS H. MARTIN—Farm-house. 10 miles; accommodate 15; terms on application; farm-cottage fitted up for boarders; the house commands a fine view of surrounding country; ½ mile from church; raise own vegetables; pure milk and butter; five minutes' walk to the lake; daily mail. Refers to P. MacDonald, 1651 Broadway, New York; Dr. J. A. Jenkins, 150 Milton Street, Brooklyn, N. Y.

Mrs. KATE WOULDRIDGE—The Laurel House. Accommodate 40 to 50; 20 rooms; adults $8 to $12, children half, transient $2; transportation from Liberty by stage, $1; private conveyance if desired; discount to season guests; raise our own vegetables; house and grounds right on the water's edge; commands finest view of the lake; piazza around house; new improvements; excellent fishing and boating; boats free; near seven churches; excellent table. Send for circular; house for sale. Refers to F. L. Jenkins, Municipal Buildings, Brooklyn, N. Y.; J. A. Macpherson, Consolidated Exchange, New York; Judge McCarthy, 49 and 51 Chambers Street, New York; and Mr. Richardson, Treasurer Park Theatre, Brooklyn, N. Y. Mrs. Wouldridge can be seen at 214 West Twenty-fifth Street, New York, up to June 15.

LEWIS F. WINTERS—Boarding-house. 9 miles; accommodate 40; rates on application; house fronts on White Lake, in full view of the water; nothing can surpass the scenery and climate in this locality; no fog, fever or ague known here; raise own vegetables; good trout, bass and pickerel fishing; one cottage with 7 rooms to let for family. References and full particulars on application.

F. B. VAN WERT—Van Wert House. Accommodate 65; rates $8 to $10; discount to families for season; this old-established summer resort is situated at the junction of Monticello and Liberty turnpikes, is near the lake, and has a well-shaded lawn together with an orchard of good fruit, with the pure breezes of the high hills of the region; there is neither malaria nor mosquitoes; house has comfortable and well-arranged family rooms, also desirable single rooms; the table is well supplied with fresh vegetables and good milk; boarders will be received on and after June 15th. City references on application.

W. VAN WERT—Willard House. Accommodate 45; adults $8 to $10, children and servants $5, transient $2; discount to season guests; situated on high ground, within 250 feet of the lake; commands a fine view of the surrounding country; 110 feet of piazza; rooms well furnished; good roads; post and telegraph offices within two minutes' walk; tennis court; croquet ground and grove well supplied with seats on lake-shore; raise own vegetables; good fishing; boats to let. Send for circular.

WILLIAM MERCER—Farm-house. Accommodate 12; adults $6.

SAMUEL KERR—Farm-house. 7 miles; accommodate 20; adults $6 to $8, children half, transient $1.25.

D. T. HOFFMAN—Boarding-house. Accommodate 60. Terms and references on application.

WILLIAM STURGIS—Boarding-house. 9 miles; accommodate 30; adults $7 to $10.

Mrs. M. A. B. WADDELL—Sunny Glade House. Accommodate 30; adults $8 to $12, children half price.

J. B. LOW—Farm-house. 8 miles; accommodate 12; terms on application; transient $1.25.

W. T. MATTISON—Farm-house. Accommodate 12; adults $5 to $6. Correspondence solicited.

PARKSVILLE, SULLIVAN CO.

A small, pretty village in the heart of the trout country, 1,582 feet above the sea. Guides can be found near the station who will, for a small consideration, accompany anglers to the best fishing grounds. We may not divulge the names of these trout streams which flow into the

124 MILES FROM NEW YORK. FARE, $3.08; EXCURSION, $5.51.

SUNDAY MORNING, WHITE LAKE.

Beaverkill, for that is the profound secret of the fishermen; but this much we can vouch for, that no man who is an expert in the art and mystery of angling, who goes to this region, will fail to secure what trout he wants, and an abundance of sport in angling for them.

PARKSVILLE STATION—Parksville Post-Office.

M. F. FISK—Farm and boarding-house. 1 mile; accommodate 60; adults $6 to $8, transient $1.50; situated on a farm of 300 acres; elevation 2,500 feet; picturesque scenery; house has been recently enlarged and refurnished; rooms large and airy; large double piazza; piano; spring water; tennis and croquet grounds; excellent table; mountain air; cool and healthy; several large lakes within a short distance of the house, where excellent fishing and boating can be had; good livery. Refers to Dr. G. A. Evans, 909 Bedford Avenue, Brooklyn, N. Y.; Edwin Simons, 20 Maiden Lane, New York.

THOMAS COSTELLO—Cranberry Lake House. 2¼ miles; accommodate 16; discount to season guests; farm is surrounded by four lakes and numerous streams; Cranberry Lake is on the farm; elevation 2,482 feet above tide water; excellent views; table abundantly supplied with fresh poultry, eggs, milk, butter, honey, maple syrup, etc.; excellent trout-fishing; boats free to guests; raise own vegetables; free transportation. Terms on application; references exchanged.

C. J. FULLER—Fuller's Farm House. ¾ mile; accommodate 15; adults $5; house situated 2 miles west of Young's Gap, the highest point on the O. & W. Railway; excellent trout and pickerel fishing; table abundantly supplied with fresh milk, butter and eggs; convenient to post-office, church and telegraph; healthy location; organ. References on application.

EDWARD COSTELLO—Farm-house. 2¼ miles; accommodate 25; discount to season guests; shady grove near house; pure running spring water; croquet ground; piano; good fishing and gunning; farm surrounded by numerous lakes and streams, well stocked with trout, bass, pickerel and perch; elevation 2,500 feet above tide-water; table well supplied with fresh poultry, eggs, milk and vegetables. Rates and references on application.

B. POST REYNOLDS—Private residence. ½ mile; accommodate 25; discount to season guests; house is large and commodious; pleasant rooms; ample shade; pure spring water; bracing mountain air; absolutely free from malaria; excellent table; good piano; fishing, gunning and livery. This village has the highest elevation of any along the line. Terms and references on application; correspondence solicited.

GEO. H. FISK (Maple Grove House)—Farm boarding-house. 1½ miles; accommodate 30; pleasantly situated; trout pond near the house, affording excellent fishing and boating; free transportation; good livery; good table, supplied with the best the country affords. Rates and references on application.

ELMER W. GRANT—Bellnaire Cottage. ¾ mile; accommodate 18; elevation 2,400 feet above the sea; spacious piazza; large, light and airy rooms; plenty of shade; abundance of fresh milk, eggs and poultry; good livery attached; free transportation; excellent trout and pickerel fishing; raise own vegetables. Rates on application; refers to Wm. T. Williams, 577 Leonard Street, Brooklyn, N. Y.; Edward Lapidge, 262 Tompkins Avenue, Brooklyn, N. Y.

WOLCOTT BRADLEY—Farm-house. ¼ mile; accommodate 16; house located in village; large lawn; plenty of shade; good running spring water; table well furnished; piano; raise own vegetables; free transportation; ¼ mile from church. Rates on application; refers to F. B. Case, 55 Liberty Street, New York.

GEO. DANZER—Farm-house. 1½ miles; accommodate 16; terms on application; free transportation; large and airy rooms; good table, well supplied with fresh butter, milk, eggs and poultry; raise own vegetables; livery attached; large wide veranda. References on application.

Miss KATE R. STEWART—Farm-house. Accommodate 20; terms on application; transportation free; table supplied with fresh milk and cream, butter, eggs, chickens, ducks, etc.; large and airy rooms; ground well shaded; piano and library; first-class livery. Refers to Mr. Jas. H Merklee, and Mr. Ernest Brown, 204 North Henry Street, Brooklyn, E. D.

H. J. COX—Farm-house. 3 miles; accommodate 10; adults $5. References on application.

J. L. PEASE—Accommodate 10; adults $6. Write for particulars.

Mrs. Elizabeth M. Rice—Farm-house. ½ mile; accommodate 10. Terms and full particulars on application.
Matthew Lare—Farm-house. 1 mile; accommodate 8; adults $7, children $3.50.
William Ross—Will take a limited number of boarders. Write for particulars.

LIVINGSTON MANOR, Sullivan Co.

129 miles from New York.
Fare, $3.21;
Excursion, $6.01.

As we step from the train at this station, we are agreeably surprised to find it so cool, even in late spring or midsummer; it is not uncommon to see snow drifts from the car windows as late as June 1st in this vicinity, and up at DeBruce, six miles away, it is claimed that ice forms on water every month in the year. This station is 129 miles from New York City, and is elevated 1,431 feet above tide-water, and was named in honor of Dr. Edward Livingston, nephew of Chancellor Livingston.

The old "Manor House," which the Doctor built, still stands, and is now a portion of the Clay Hotel, but a few steps from the station. The tourist, whether he comes here for a few days, fishing or hunting or for a two-months' stay, will find the best of accommodations at the numerous public houses, or in the homes of private families. The Little Beaverkill and Willowemoc streams unite their waters here. At the junction of these two rivers, and entirely surrounded by water, is an island of some forty acres, known as Sherwood's Grove, a favorite and popular resort.

The tourist is now in the very heart of the far-famed Beaverkill trout-fishing grounds, and during the hunting season can, if he chooses, bring down, with a well-directed shot, perhaps a bear or deer. Partridge-shooting is good on the hills overlooking the village. The growth of Livingston Manor has been so rapid as to astonish even the most sanguine, having increased in the last decade from 100 to nearly 1,000, at the time of taking the last census. This section of Sullivan County was for many years the El Dorado of the lumberman and the tanner. And now that sawdust and tan bark are no longer allowed to pollute the numerous fine trout streams about here, and together with the fact that the Company, assisted by private enterprise, have for many years been stocking these streams with vast numbers of fish from the State Hatchery, the number and size of the fish are increasing rapidly.

City people who are looking for a quiet spot "far from the madding crowd" and the shriek of the locomotive, will leave the Ontario & Western here and find stages ready to carry them in the Shin Creek region, eight miles away over the hills. This is the Lew Beach Post-

ALONG THE MONGAUP.

JUNCTION OF DELAWARE AND BEAVERKILL RIVERS AT EAST BRANCH STATION.

office, and here also will be found the finest of trout-fishing in the Beaverkill and the many excellent trout streams that empty into it.

LIVINGSTON MANOR STATION—Livingston Manor Post-Office.

LIVINGSTON MANOR—Hotel. ¼ mile; accommodate 80; 52 rooms; adults $6 to $8, children reduction, transient $1.50; stages leave this hotel after the arrival of trains for Shin Creek, Beaverkill, De Bruce and Willowemoc; very pleasantly situated; charming and diversified scenery; spring water; raise our own vegetables; excellent trout-fishing; all kinds of game; convenient to church; excellent table; desirable summer resort; this house has been greatly enlarged by an addition of 75 feet by 30, making it one of the most pleasant and convenient hotels in the country, with private sitting-rooms and bath-rooms, and in the winter the building is heated throughout with steam. References on application. W. L. McPherson, proprietor.

D. B. MUNSON—Farm-house. 2½ miles; accommodate 12; rates on application, transient $1; a beautiful shady yard; good spring water running through the house; table supplied with the best the country affords; excellent trout-fishing; good fox, rabbit and partridge shooting; 1 mile to church; romantic walks and drives; home comforts. References and full particulars furnished on application.

WEBSTER SHERWOOD—Village residence. ½ mile; accommodate 15; this residence is new, handsomely furnished and located on high ground; shade and ornamental trees; pure spring water on both floors of house, also at stable, which is in best condition for horses. Rates and references on application. This is a very desirable home for those seeking quiet and rest. Will rent this handsome residence and buildings for the season, or sell at reasonable figure.

J. TERWILLIGER & E. L. BENTON—"The P. H. Woolsey House." Expressly for summer guests; five minutes' walk from depot and post-office; accommodate 100; adults $5 to $7, children $3 to $5, transient $1; first-class board; rooms large and airy; good spring water on each floor; plenty of shade; first-class livery at reasonable terms; excellent gunning and fishing; free transportation. Refers to F. H. Weed, 295 Pearl Street, New York; George F. Armstrong, Room 4, Garfield Building, Brooklyn, N. Y.

JOHN C. HORNBECK–Sturdevant House. Near station; accommodate 30; adults $7 to $10, children $3 50 to $4.50, transient $1.50; pleasantly situated; fine views; large verandas; first-class table; no liquors sold; a very quiet resort for guests; plenty of shade, good water, and every convenience; the proprietor being familiar with all the fishing-grounds of the Willowemoc and Beaverkill can furnish guests and transients all information and transportation to reach the best fishing-grounds. Correspondence solicited and promptly answered.

WM. P. ROSE—Farm-house. 2 miles; accommodate 15; adults $5, children on application; will meet guests at station with carriage, free; this house is bounded on two sides by trout streams in which there is the best of fishing; perfectly healthy location; surrounded by maple shade trees; plenty of fruit in season; table supplied with the best farm products. Refers to V. Trowbridge, 58 Lincoln Place, Brooklyn, N. Y., and John Drake, P. O. box 194, New York.

To RENT—An unfurnished cottage at Liberty Falls; modern architecture; complete in all its appointments; situated ¼ mile from Liberty Falls Station; five sleeping-rooms; accommodate about 8 people; splendid fishing in the vicinity. Will rent for season or sell at moderate price; apply to Webster Sherwood, Livingston Manor, N. Y.

OSCAR STURDEVANT—Riverside Farm House. 3½ miles; accommodate 12; adults $6, children half, transient $1; discount to season guests; situated on high ground; pure spring water; fine grove a short distance from the Willowemoc river; raise our own vegetables; good trout-fishing and gunning; first-class livery; 2 miles from church.

W. J. UNKENHOLZ—Accommodate 6. Write for terms and particulars.

S. S. VOORHEES—Beaverkill Beach House. 7 miles; accommodate 20; adults $6 to $7, transient $1.

LIVINGSTON MANOR STATION—Lew Beach Post-Office.

ABEL L. SPRAGUE—Farm-house. 8 miles; accommodate 12; terms reasonable; raise own vegetables; ample shade; spacious piazza; good table; mineral well; excellent trout-fishing; daily mail; convenient to church; charming scenery; pleasant location. References on application.

JOHN SHAFFER—Formerly Slater's Mountain Lake House. 13 miles; accommodate 20; terms on application; 1,800 feet elevation; lake near house; excellent bass-fishing; boats free to guests; picturesque scenery; liberal table; pure bracing air. References on application.

JAMES M. BARNHART—Farm-house. 12½ miles; accommodate 14; terms on application; house is situated on the banks of the Beaverkill; healthy location; picturesque scenery; excellent trout-fishing; pure spring water; raise own vegetables; charming surroundings. References on application.

LIVINGSTON MANOR STATION—De Bruce Post-Office.

W. F. ROYCE—Boarding and farm-house. 6 miles; accommodate 15; adults $8 to $12, transient $1.50; moderate charge for meeting guests at depot; located at the junction of the Willowemoc and Mongaup trout streams; abundance of fine lawn; tennis court and croquet grounds; forest lands; running spring water; have leased for a term of years the fishing-grounds of Mrs. Henry, including the Spring Brook on the Mongaup, also fishing-grounds of Fish & Hammond on the Willowemoc, fishing privileges without extra charge; good livery. References on application.

M. M. COOPER—Boarding and farm-house. 6 miles; accommodate 50; adults $7 to $10, transient $1.50; conveyance will meet guests; delighful scenery, affording romantic walks and drives; abundant shade; attractive grounds; large rooms; bountiful table; two new cottages with rooms for lodging, or will let cottages for season; best trout-fishing in the county. Refers to Dr. R. E. Van Gieson, 94 Kent Street, Brooklyn, N. Y., and H. B. Riggs, 26 Broadway, New York.

THOMAS O'KEEFE—Farm-house. 6 miles; accommodate 6; adults $5 to $7.

LIVINGSTON MANOR STATION—Beaverkill Post-Office.

Miss M. W. STONE—Clear Lake Cottage. Accommodate 30; adults $7 and upwards; transportation $1; within ten minutes' walk of the Beaverkill; boating and black-bass fishing at lake near house; croquet grounds; no mosquitoes; good food; poultry in abundance. Refers to Mr. Frank Rudd, 102 Broadway, New York; Rev. T. K. Beecher, Elmira, N. Y., and Mrs. E. McGukin, 283 West 72d Street, New York.

Mrs. H. ELLSWORTH—Maple Grove House. Accommodate 20; adults $6.

R. G. ROOSA (Willowemoc Post-Office)—Willowemoc Hotel. Accommodate 20. Terms and full particulars on application.

ROCKLAND, SULLIVAN CO.,

Is distant from New York City 136 miles, and has an elevation above sea-level of 1,284 feet. Here we have the twin villages of Rockland and Roscoe, the last-named being in the vicinity of the station, and named after the late Roscoe Conkling. The first-named village is one mile away from the station, and but little of it can be seen from passing trains. The combined population of these two villages cannot be less than 1,000, and is rapidly increasing. Those in search of "a home among the mountains," during the heated term, will have no trouble in making a selection from among the many who have made preparations to accommodate the summer boarder. The Willowemoc and Beaverkill

136 MILES FROM NEW YORK.
FARE, $3.42;
EXCURSION, $6.23.

EAST BRANCH OF THE DELAWARE.

proper meet here, about a quarter of a mile below the railroad station; and for some years past the trout-fishing in both of these rivers has been excellent, some of the best native fishermen preferring these large streams to the numerous smaller trout brooks that are to be found on all sides.

Russell Pond, five miles from Rockland Village, is the Mecca to which all true disciples of Izaak Walton turn their steps sooner or later, and it can be reached more easily from this point than any other. This is by all odds the finest trout lake in the State, nestled among the Delaware County hills, and more than 2,000 feet above tide-water.

ROCKLAND STATION—Rockland Post-Office.

B. F. HARDENBERGH—Farm-house. 3 miles; accommodate 20; adults $5 to $7, transient $1; headquarters for fishing parties; a large club-house on the premises; this house is located in the woods; pure mountain air; table well supplied with fresh milk, butter and eggs; free transportation if guests remain more than one week; best fishing for many miles around; good livery; first-class table. City references and full particulars on application.

AHIRA GREEN—Hotel. 1 mile; accommodate 50; adults $7, children $4; free transportation; maple grove and croquet grounds; shady walks along the Beaverkill; post and telegraph office convenient; six lakes within six miles affording first-class pickerel-fishing; good partridge, wild duck, rabbit and fox shooting; good livery; table supplied with all the delicacies of the season. Refers to H. H. Behrman, 221 Ross Street, Brooklyn, and others on application.

Mrs. ELEANOR H. JAGGER—1 mile; adults $5; particulars on application.

JEFFERSON CAMPBELL—Near depot; accommodate 10; adults $7, children $3; good fishing in the Beaverkill and Willowemoc rivers; good gunning; first-class livery; five minutes' walk to church; large and comfortable rooms; liberal table. References and full particulars on application.

LOUIS SIPPLE—Boarding-house. ¼ mile; accommodate 15; adults $10, children $5; first-class trout-fishing; good gunning for small game; nicely situated; healthy location; pure air; plenty of shade; excellent table; romantic walks and drives. Correspondence solicited.

ROCKLAND STATION—Roscoe Post-Office.

THOMAS S. SEELEY—Dodge's Hotel. Five minutes' walk; accommodate 12; adults $6 to $7, transient $1; discount to season guests; surroundings are very pretty and attractive; excellent trout-fishing; raise own vegetables; good gunning; fine livery attached. References and full particulars on application.

A. J. BENNETT—Farm-house. At station; accommodate 20; adults $7, children $5; discount to season guests; excellent trout-fishing in the Willowemoc; mill pond covering three acres for boating; plenty of shade; cold running spring water; free transportation; near churches; first-class table. References and full particulars on application.

COOK'S FALLS, DELAWARE CO.,

Situated on the Beaverkill, 1,184 feet above the sea, is the first station in Delaware County (the post-office is Butternut Grove) and derives its name from a fall in the Beaverkill, on whose banks the village stands, and can be considered the entrance to the "Midland Trosachs," and it is well worth ten years of city life to spend a week fishing or hunting in this

141 MILES FROM NEW YORK. FARE, $3.87; EXCURSION, $6.63.

neighborhood. Four miles south of this place is Long Pond, one of the largest bodies of water in Sullivan County. The water here is deep and well adapted to the growth of the speckled or native trout, some having been caught that weighed three pounds. Several years ago the Company stocked these waters with lake trout that have already grown to considerable size and are now frequently caught. One mile below, Russell brook unites with the river, and, like the pond from which it takes its rise, is famous for the excellent fishing that it affords.

COOK'S FALLS STATION—Butternut Grove Post-Office.

PARKER COOK—Farm-house. Near depot; accommodate 20; adults $5, children under twelve $3, transient $1; new building with four large sleeping-rooms attached has been erected this season; excellent fishing and gunning; boats and fishing-tackle free to guests; free transportation; abundance of fresh milk, butter, eggs, maple syrup, honey, fruits of all kinds in season; raise own vegetables; within two minutes' walk of church; good livery at reasonable rates. Refers to Wm. Merker, 200 South Fourth Street, Brooklyn, N. Y.; J. H. Andrews, 312 South Fifth Street, Brooklyn, N. Y., and Wm. Sheller, 326 Broadway, New York.

S. E. WORMUTH—Hotel. ¼ mile; accommodate 10; adults $4.50 to $5, children $3.

VIRGIL A. FRANCISCO—Will take a limited number of summer boarders. Rates and full particulars on application.

COOK'S FALLS STATION—Horton Post-Office.

B. F. KEENE—Farm-house. 5 miles; accommodate 10; adults $5, children $3; discount to season guests; raise own vegetables; pure running spring water; plenty of shade; abundance of fresh milk, butter and eggs; good gunning and fishing; free transportation. References on application.

EAST BRANCH, DELAWARE CO.

In Nature's voluminous album of beauty there are few, if any,

| 161 MILES FROM NEW YORK. |
| FARE, $3.87; |
| EXCURSION, $6.75. |

more attractive pages than the County of Delaware, the most picturesque portions of which are interwoven with the serpentine course of the east and west branches of the Delaware river, which have their sources respectively in the towns of Roxbury and Harpersfield and flow parallel in a southwesterly direction across the county, uniting at Hancock. These rivers are lined their entire length with precipitous mountains, rich farm lands and pretty villages, showing some new wonder of nature at every bend. They are Delaware's "lines of beauty," and the county is well adorned with these bright jewels threaded across her fair breast. Then there is the Beaverkill river, which has its source near the head-waters of the east branch of the Delaware, and empties its waters into that river at East Branch, its course being traversed several miles by the N. Y., O. & W. Railway. Though smaller than its sister rivers, it is quite a Cinderella in its primitive beauty. It is separated from the east branch in its entire course by a long

DELAWARE AT EAST BRANCH.

spur of the Catskill, which ends abruptly at the junction of those rivers, at East Branch, in a knob known as Christopher Mountain— the Pike's Peak of Delaware County.

A HANDSOME COUNTRY VILLA—"THE PINES."

It is at the foot of this mountain on a small promontory, between and some fifty feet above the rivers and four or five hundred feet from their junction, that Gen. W. Martin, a man closely identified with many of the leading public and private enterprises of Delaware County, built his handsome residence.

"The Pines," a name very appropriately bestowed, since the side of the mountain in the immediate rear of the house is covered with a rich growth of tall pines; and it may well be added here that "The Pines," with its wealth of nature's beauty as complemented by the art of man, is the most romantic, wildest, prettiest place in this section of the State.

EAST BRANCH STATION—East Branch Post-Office.

WILLIAM MARTIN—"The Pines." ¼ mile; accommodate 20; terms $7 to $10; trout and bass fishing; boating and bathing. This handsome villa is situated at the foot of the mountain, on a small promontory between and 50 feet above the rivers Delaware and Beaverkill, and has recently been completed; the house contains 17 sleeping-rooms, 2 bath-rooms and water closet, hot and cold water, fireplaces, broad piazza, and all modern improvements; the scenery is said to be the finest in this section of the State; views taken from the house will be found in this book. References on application.

A. J. FRANCISCO & MILLER—Boarding and farm-house. ¼ mile; accommodate 40; adults $7 to $8, children $5, transient $2; discount to season guests; wild and rugged mountain scenery; fine boating; picturesque and attractive section, situated at the junction of the Delaware and Beaverkill rivers; trout-fishing unsurpassed; plenty of game in the vicinity; boats free. Refers to E. P. Benedict, 171 Broadway, New York; Thos. R. Withers, 432 Ninth Avenue, New York; E. C. Henry, 383 Eighth Street, Jersey City, N. J., and Wm. D. Utley, 34 and 36 Wall Street, New York.

GEORGE W. JONES—Boarding-house. Near depot; accommodate 12; adults $7 to $10, children half, transient $2.

EAST BRANCH STATION—Harvard Post-Office.

O. P. SUTTON—Farm-house. 5 miles; accommodate 12; free transportation one way; rooms large and airy; raise own vegetables; excellent trout-fishing; boats free to guests; good woodcock and partridge shooting; terms on application; good table. Refers to H. R. Miller, West New Brighton, Staten Island, N. Y., and A. L. Powell, 129 Pearl Street, New York.

DOWNSVILLE, DELAWARE CO.,

Twelve miles northeast of East Branch, and communicating with it by daily stage. Situated on the head-waters of the east branch of the Delaware river, with a population of about 600. Splendid hunting and fishing.

EAST BRANCH STATION—Downsville Post-Office.

NATHAN S. BOYD—Accommodate 4; adults $5. Particulars on application.

EAST BRANCH STATION—Colchester Post-Office.

J. H. BULL—Pleasant country home. Correspondence solicited.

HANCOCK JUNCTION STATION—Cadosia Post-Office.

JOHN MCGRANAGHAN—Hotel. At station; accommodate 18; 20 sleeping-rooms; adults $6, children $3, transient $2; reduction to season guests; excellent fishing in the numerous streams in the vicinity; charming surroundings; high elevation; bracing air; picturesque scenery; absolutely free from malaria; a very desirable spot for those seeking a quiet and healthy home; fine livery attached; first-class table. Write for particulars.

JOHN SCHAEFER—Hotel and boarding-house. ¼ mile; accommodate 50; adults $5 to $7, children reduction; situated on high ground, commanding a magnificent view of the surrounding country for many miles; good healthy location; first-class table; well-shaded lawns; abundance of fresh milk, butter and eggs. References and full particulars on application.

HANCOCK, DELAWARE CO.,

Is located 1,005 feet above the sea, and is an enterprising village of 2,500 inhabitants. There are four churches in the village, Methodist, Congregational, Baptist and Catholic, and a very fine union free school and academy. It is but thirty minutes' ride from the Ontario & Western's newly opened summer resort, Preston Park, Wayne County, Pa. It is fast coming into popular favor as a summer home for city people. Shanly's new hotel at Hancock is one of the best of the southern tier, being elegantly fitted up. The village is neat and pleasant, with the best of stone walks, and picturesque drives. It was Hancock which the author, N. P. Willis, used to annually visit, and "Point Mountain" and "Chehocton" (the Indian name for Hancock, signifying the "wedding of the waters") figure prominently in his delightful sketches. The east and west branches of the Delaware unite here and form the Delaware river. Bass and trout fishing are exceptionally good around Hancock, particularly the former. There are a number of good hotels and boarding-houses offering pleasant accommodations at reasonable rates.

160 MILES FROM NEW YORK.
FARE, $4.14;
EXCURSION, $6.75.

HANCOCK STATION—Hancock Post-Office.

JOHN SHANLY—Hotel. ¼ mile; accommodate 100; adults $7 to $12, children $5 to $7, transient $2.

Mrs. S. A. SANDS—Would like a limited number of boarders; quiet location. Write for particulars.

HANCOCK JUNCTION.

Scranton Division.

Leaving Hancock, the Scranton Division crosses the Delaware river and runs through the beautiful lake region of Wayne County. In the two counties of Wayne and Susquehanna are 127 of these lovely mountain lakes, the greater number of which have been stocked with gamy bass and pickerel, furnishing sport dear to the heart of the fisherman who is almost always sure of good fishing in the clear water of their glacial ponds.

The road winds along the conical form of Sugar Loaf, and by the rocky slopes of Ararat. A few miles west of Ararat is the highest railroad pass in the United States east of the Rocky Mountains, being some 2,500 feet above tide-water, and here, in the fierce blasts of winter, railroad men encounter storms of snow and wind which frequently delay the long, heavy coal trains for hours at a time, and to these wild storms they gave the lively name of "Ararat thaws."

PRESTON PARK CLUB-HOUSE.

STARLIGHT, WAYNE CO., PA.

Starlight is eight miles from the main line and on an elevation of commanding outlook. About it are Lizard Lake, Preston Lake, Island Pond, Four-Mile and Star Ponds, all of which afford excellent fishing, and some of which can be seen from the station.

PRESTON PARK, WAYNE CO., PA.

Delightfully situated on the eastern summit of the Moosic range, 2,500 feet above sea-level, surrounded by beautiful spring lakes stocked with game fish. The Preston Park Association (Limited) has erected a handsome $10,000 club-house for use of its members and transients. Cottages are being erected; sail and row-boat livery attached; two miles from O. & W. Railway depot; 'bus meets all trains; only five hours from New York. Address, Mrs. E. P. Webb (housekeeper), Preston Park, Wayne Co., Pa., or Secretary of Preston Park Association, Carbondale, Pa.

COMO, WAYNE CO., PA.

Probably at no point along the Scranton Division is there presented to the eye a more truly magnificent outlook than that which greets the eye of the traveler as the train pulls out from Como on its way northward. There with the naked eye can be seen the Seven-Mile Pond, Como Lake, Spruce Pond, Sly and Long Ponds, and several other but smaller placid sheets of water with their settings of sloping meadows and hills and forests.

COMO STATION—Lakin Post-Office, Wayne County, Pa.

L. W. ROOD—Farm-house. ¼ mile; accommodate 16; adults $6, children $5, transient $1; house pleasantly situated, in sight of Como Station: free transportation to and from depot; raise own vegetables; excellent table; good fishing and gunning; discount to season guests; picturesque scenery. References on application.

G L. DAVALL—Will take summer boarders. 1½ miles. Rates and full particulars on application.

Mrs. H. H. BUDD—Private house. At depot; accommodate 2 young men, $4. Write for particulars.

JOHN RANDALL (Lake Como Post-Office)—Private boarding-house. Accommodate 15; adults $7.

POYNTELLE, WAYNE CO., PA.

Surrounded with the lakes and ponds of Wayne County, one of which, Five-Mile Lake, is the dividing line, the waters on the east flowing to the Delaware, and on the west to the Lackawanna river.

POYNTELLE STATION—Poyntelle Post-Office, Wayne County, Pa.

JOHN T. FULKERSON—Hotel. Accommodate 30; adults $7 to $10; reasonable discount for children, transient $1.50; discount to season guests; house situated on the summit, 2,000 feet above tide-water, on dividing waters of the Delaware and Susquehanna rivers; it is surrounded with timber on all sides, with a fine grove leading from the house to Lake Poyntelle, about 200 yards distant; raise our own vegetables; fresh butter and milk; good fishing in Poyntelle, Bone, Spruce, Independent, and Big and Little Hickory lakes—bass, pickerel, perch, etc.; the streams abound with speckled trout; these lakes and streams are within one mile of the house; boats and fishing-tackle free; excellent gunning—pheasants, rabbits, squirrels and ducks; livery attached; 1½ miles from church. Refers to J. D. Brannan, Merchant; J. E. Tiffany, Druggist, and Dr. Noble, Pleasant Mount, Wayne Co., Pa.

BELMONT, WAYNE CO., PA.

A distinctly agricultural town and the centre of a large and prosperous farming community. In the vicinity are numerous lakes and ponds affording excellent fishing.

178 MILES FROM NEW YORK. LIMITED FARE, $4.35. EXCURSION, $6.75.

PLEASANT MOUNT, WAYNE CO., PA.

Like Belmont, an agricultural village, and the surrounding section offers many desirable summer homes. Like it, also, in having in its neighborhood several lakes and ponds.

183 MILES FROM NEW YORK. LIMITED FARE, $4.35; EXCURSION, $6.75.

UNIONDALE, SUSQUEHANNA CO., PA.

Uniondale contains about 300 inhabitants, and is one of the prettiest villages in Susquehanna County. It is twenty-eight miles from Scranton, twelve from Carbondale and six from Forest City. Uniondale is the centre of an agricultural region, is prettily laid out, and is surrounded by picturesque hills, among which are numerous ponds and lakes well stocked with fish.

186 MILES FROM NEW YORK. LIMITED FARE, $4.35; EXCURSION, $6.75.

FOREST CITY, SUSQUEHANNA CO., PA.

Forest City is located near the head-waters of the Lackawanna river, and is at the extreme northeastern edge of the Pennsylvania anthracite coal-measure. The borough contains about 2,500 inhabitants, and is engaged principally in coal-mining. Three miles away is Crystal Lake. West and north is a wild mountainous country affording the finest hunting and fishing found in the State. It contains six good hotels and private houses where summer boarders are entertained.

191 MILES FROM NEW YORK. LIMITED FARE, $4.35; EXCURSION, $6.75.

CARBONDALE, SUSQUEHANNA CO., PA.

Carbondale, the pioneer city of the Lackawanna Valley, was settled in 1829-30 by the Wurtz Brothers, who were the officers and agents of the Delaware & Hudson Canal Company. Here is a thriving city of some 10,000 or 12,000 inhabitants, with manufactories and shops and all the evidences of a prosperous mining city. Here, too, the celebrated Gravity Road starts out to climb the mountain to Fairview, a summer resort on the very top of the Moosic, 2,200 feet above tidewater. The view from the observatory at this point is one never to be forgotten. The eye ranges over miles and miles of wooded hill and dale, interspersed with gleaming bodies of water, where nestle mountain lakes, and rich farming lands dotted with houses and orchards and fields of waving grain. Nineteen of these beautiful lakes can be counted from the observatory in favorable weather. WHITE BRIDGE, JERMYN, ARCHBALD, WINTON, PECKVILLE, OLYPHANT, DICKSON, THROOP, PROVIDENCE and PARK PLACE are stations in the almost continuous village stretching from Carbondale to Scranton, and all surrounded by the great coal-breakers of the mining companies.

CARBONDALE STATION—Carbondale Post-Office.

Mrs. M. H. MUNLY—Boarding-house.   Accommodate 15; $4.50 per week.   Correspondence solicited.

SCRANTON, LACKAWANNA CO.

Scranton, the county seat of Lackawanna County, has well been called a Western City in an Eastern State. Started in 1847 as a little village about the iron-works of Henry & Co., by 1850 it had a population of 3,000; in 1860 this had increased to 9,000; in 1870 it had grown to 35,000; then came the depressing years between 1873 and 1877, when men left the coal-fields seeking work elsewhere, and yet by 1880 it had grown to 45,000; since then all the evidence at hand of directories and the most conservative estimates place its population at not less than 100,000. Where but a comparatively few years ago the north winds sighed among the pine and hemlock branches, to-day are to be found streets paved with sheet asphalt and lined on either side with handsome houses, the homes of Scranton's prosperous business men. In addition to its great advantages as a manufacturing and business centre, it is also one of the pleasantest summer resorts in the country. Here the nights in the summer are rarely ever oppressively warm, and from here as a centre daily excursions can be made to numerous points of interest scattered all around the valley and up and down the mountain ranges that hem it in on either side.

Scranton produces more steel rails within its limits than any other city in the world. Its two great mills turn out an average of over 1,000 tons of steel rails for every working-day in the year, and the light from the blast furnaces and steel converters casts a brilliant glow upon the horizon, night after night, year in and year out, while he fiery shower of sparks emitted by the huge converters at the end of each turn form a never-ending source of delight to the visitors, who nightly visit the steel mills to see a finer exhibition of fireworks than a Fourth of July display affords.

Its Secretary is always ready to furnish any information in regard to its resources.

Valley of the Delaware.

APEX STATION—Cannonsville, N. Y., Post-Office.

Mrs. JOSEPHINE SEYMOUR—Farm-house. 5 miles; accommodate 15; adults $5, children $3.50, transient $1.

R. G. McGIBBON—Chestnut Point. Opens June 15th, 1892. Terms and full particulars on application.

ROCK RIFT, DELAWARE CO.

Returning to the main line after leaving Hancock Junction, the road for five miles makes a rapid ascent of the mountain dividing these streams, and passes over it at Apex, 1,462 feet above the sea, to the western face, along the precipitous side of which the roadway is hewn out of solid granite and gneiss. In this vicinity we pass the most striking scenery upon the entire road. Rock Rift is the only station which arrests the downward flight of the train. About half-way down the mountain the eye of the traveler is greeted with a glorious landscape, equaling the view of the famous Starrucca Valley. The west, or Mohawk, branch of the Delaware comes in sight, threading its way in its narrow and rocky channel far below, while its western bank is a lofty and almost perpendicular wall of rock. If this passage of the west branch through these rocky walls occurred in any of the rivers west of the Mississippi, it would be dignified with the high-sounding title of canyon. After descending the mountain, the train crosses the west branch of the Delaware river, and reaches

[172 MILES FROM NEW YORK. FARE, $4.50; EXCURSION, $7.75.]

APEX or ROCK RIFT STATION—Carpenter's Eddy Post-Office.

W. A. NOBLE—Pine Hill Farm. New farm-house; rooms high; windows large; piazza; bath-room; running water; fine views of Delaware and valley for four miles; farm livery; reasonable rates; adults $8, children under 10 years $5. References and particulars on application.

WALTON, DELAWARE CO.

Walton is the largest village in Delaware County, situated on the Delaware river, amid most beautiful mountain scenery, 1,220 feet above the sea. On the east stands the western range of the Catskill system, and on the

[180 MILES FROM NEW YORK. FARE, $4.74; EXCURSION, $6.15.]

ALONG THE DELHI BRANCH.

west the less rugged hills, which compose the water-shed between the Delaware and the Susquehanna rivers. No prettier or more thriving village exists in this section of the State. With its six churches, academy, village hall, fine residences and model stores, its beautifully shaded and thoroughly flagged streets, its charming drives and noted trout streams, its public water-works, supplying pure spring water, its comfortable hotels and private boarding-houses, it offers a choice summer retreat to those seeking rest and refreshment from the heat and bustle of city life, and among its 2,500 inhabitants the visitor may find all varieties of social life and pleasure.

WALTON STATION—Walton Post-Office.

Mrs. J. Martin—Private residence. ½ mile; accommodate 8; 5 rooms; adults $6 and $7, children $4, transient $1; discount to season guests; 'bus meets all trains; large, airy rooms, neatly furnished; plenty of shade; desirable location; abundance of milk, eggs and fruit; six churches within five minutes' walk; first-class livery and drives; trout, bass and pickerel fishing; see description of Walton elsewhere. Refers to C. W. M. Sumner, 325 Nostrand Avenue, Brooklyn, N. Y., and W. J. Martin, Delmonico Building, 56 Beaver Street, New York City.

Mrs. Maggie Smith—Private house. Accommodate 6; adults $5, children $3; adults preferred; house situated on an eminence overlooking the village; fifteen minutes' walk from post-office and depot; abundance of fresh butter, milk and eggs, which are produced on the farm. References on application.

Walter G. Thompson—Farm-house. 1½ miles; accommodate 6; adults $5.

Mrs. A. D. Gould—Village residence. ¼ mile; accommodate 6. Write for particulars.

WALTON STATION—Loomis Post-Office.

Edwin Wakeman—Farm-house. 4 miles; accommodate 15; adults $5, transient 75 cents; free transportation; discount to season guests; trout stream running through farm; plenty of shade; pure air; raise own vegetables; large and airy rooms; very healthy location. Refers to David W. Lewis & Co, 177 and 179 Chambers Street, New York.

WALTON STATION—Beerston Post-Office.

Ephraim S. Beers—Farm-house. ½ mile; accommodate 12; 7 sleeping-rooms; adults $7, children according to age; discount to season guests; new house; nicely located; very healthy pond 40 feet from the house; boats free to guests; hammocks, swings, grove, etc.; excellent trout-fishing; good woodchuck and squirrel hunting; first-class livery attached. Refers to H. D. Garrison, Walton, N. Y.

Smith H. Goodrich—Farm-house. 2½ miles; accommodate 4; adults $5.

COAL-BREAKERS.

The Delhi Branch.

At Walton the Delhi Branch to Delhi leaves the main line. It is seventeen miles in length, and for its entire distance follows the west branch of the Delaware, as it winds through the narrow, exquisitely lovely valley, with its fertile mountain sides dotted here and there with groups of "sweet-breathed kine," and with fields of green and gold lying in between. To the lover of pastoral scenes no more enjoyable ride than that through this valley could be taken. The first station on the branch is at

HAMDEN, Delaware Co.

A busy, breezy hamlet, 1,450 feet above the sea, and the centre of as fine a grazing country as can be found in the State.

189 MILES FROM NEW YORK. FARE, $5.00; EXCURSION, $8.25.

HAMDEN STATION—Hamden Post-Office.

FOR SALE—A very desirable property in the village of Hamden, located on the N. Y., O. & W. Railway. This property consists of a fine residence and 40 acres of land. The house cost to build at least $10,000, and is peculiarly adapted to a summer home, or could be changed into a summer hotel. Address D. A. Shaw, Hamden, N. Y.

HOUSE TO RENT—One mile from depot; either furnished or unfurnished; 9 large bedrooms; good running water; large grounds; good fruit; carriage-house. Correspondence solicited. Address Delia F. Bostwick, Hamden, N. Y.

IRA SMITH—Youman's Cottage, hotel and boarding-house. ½ mile; accommodate 20; adults $6 to $8, children half; free transportation; 'bus to all trains; one of the most pleasantly situated boarding-houses on the Delhi Branch; only a short distance from telegraph and post-office; butter, eggs, milk and vegetables supplied by farm connected with hotel; best of fishing; good livery attached; near the base-ball grounds; best amateur nine in Delaware County.

SAMUEL BRICE'S HOTEL—¼ mile; accommodate 20. Rates on application.

Mrs. JULIA A. MALLORY (Hawley's Post-Office)—Farm-house. ¼ mile; accommodate 10; adults $5; gentlemen preferred.

DE LANCEY, Delaware Co.

A very pretty village, with two churches, school-house, etc. There are here some boarding-houses very pleasantly situated, where summer homes can be found free from the annoyances or troubles which make existence a burden in lower and less beautiful lands.

191 MILES FROM NEW YORK. FARE, $5.05; EXCURSION, $8.40.

DE LANCEY STATION—De Lancey Post-Office.

J. C. WANNAMAKER—Will rent for the summer a furnished cottage. Write for particulars.

DELHI, DELAWARE CO.

Delhi, the county seat of Delaware County, is particularly adapted by natural beauty, elevation and climate for a summer resort, and is highly recommended by eminent physicians for those seeking rest and recreation in the country during the summer. It is located 1,453 feet above tide-water, absolutely free from malaria and mosquitoes, and is one of the most beautiful towns in the State. The west branch of the Delaware passes to the west of the village, and the Little Delaware, after forming its eastern boundary, bisects it and joins the parent stream about a mile below. Surrounded on all sides by spurs of the Catskills, which lose themselves in the most romantic valleys, one can drive in any direction and have at every step a shifting panorama of the wildest scenery. The walks in every direction are very attractive, the streets broad, shady and with excellent sidewalks. The churches, public buildings and private residences are elegant, the people intelligent and refined. The village is supplied with water and protected from fire by an excellent system of water-works, the water being brought from a lake or tarn high up in the overhanging hills. Beside the larger, there are several smaller streams well stocked with trout and other kinds of fish, which afford capital sport for the angler, the streams being annually replenished with young trout from the State Hatchery.

THE HEALTHFULNESS OF DELHI.

Delhi and vicinity are remarkably healthy. Situated in a narrow valley, at an elevation of 1,458 feet, with numerous streams and avenues for drainage, makes it impossible to obtain low, flat land or local accumulations for the development of miasmatic or malarial difficulties, especially with the ever-changing wind currents. Another reason for its healthfulness is the cleanliness of its dwellings and streets. These, together with the intelligence of its inhabitants in regard to sanitary laws and their importance, all contribute to establishing a better degree of health than prevails in other localities, as well as mitigating the severity and dangers of the epidemics of the diseases of children and unavoidable sickness. This is established from the fact that this vicinity has never been subjected to the severe epidemics that have prevailed in other parts of the county and State.

An inspection of the vital statistics of the town of Delhi from 1884 (the time of the commencement of such registration) to the close of 1888—four years—shows that there were 251 deaths in a population of 3,000, or a yearly average per cent. of 1.67. Of these 251 deaths there were three from bronchitis, all under one year; there

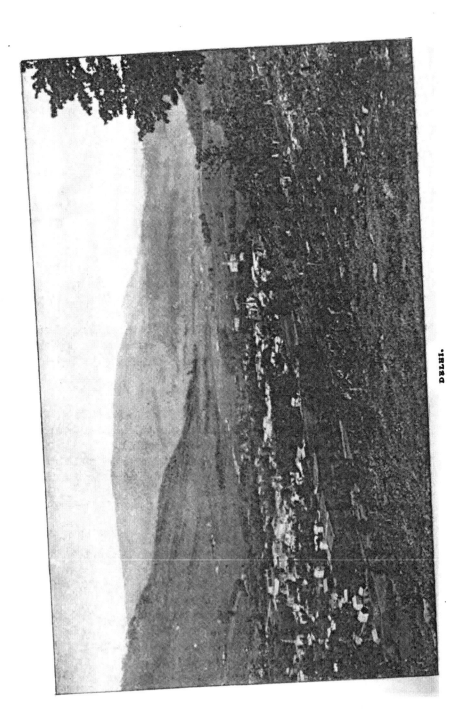

DELHI.

were nineteen deaths from pneumonia, of which one-half were over sixty-five; of measles, one; of scarlet fever, none in four years; of diphtheria, one, and only two deaths in all this time from typhoid fever—and there is no more correct criterion of the healthfulness of a place than the prevalence or absence of diphtheria and typhoid fever. So we see that the statistics fully corroborate the fact that Delhi is one of the healthiest localities to be found anywhere.

DELHI STATION—Delhi Post-Office.

Mrs. JOHN HUTSON—Delhi Hall. ½ mile; accommodate 40; three-story building; entirely new furnishings throughout; 40 feet above the village, overlooking the Delaware river; good spring water; bath-rooms; large windows and airy rooms; extensive grounds, nicely laid out; abundance of shade; scenery unsurpassed; croquet and tennis ground; hunting, boating and fishing; raise our own vegetables; near churches, telegraph, telephone and post-office. Best references on application; correspondence solicited.

R. D. W. KIFF—American Hotel. ½ mile; accommodate 30; rates on application; transient $2; free transportation; modern improvements; splendidly located; trout, bass and pickerel fishing; good livery; fine drives; raise our own vegetables; shady walks; no mosquitoes or malaria; convenient to churches, telegraph and post-office; satisfaction guaranteed. References on application.

T. D. KINGSTON—Hotel Kingston. ⅛ mile; accommodate 50; 50 rooms; very moderate terms on application; free transportation from depot; house has been remodeled completely—every room newly papered, painted, and all furniture and bedding entirely new; it is one of the leading hotels in central New York; livery connected with the house; good rooms; liberal table; plenty of milk, eggs and vegetables; splendid roads; splendid fishing and gunning. References on application.

F. H. GRIFFIS—Edgerton House. ¼ mile; accommodate 100; rates on application; free transportation; large and pleasant hotel, with airy rooms and first-class table; good livery accommodation; splendid drives and walks; good trout-fishing and shooting. Refers to J. S. McWilliams, 41 Broadway, and H. C. McDonald, 144 East 41st Street, New York.

N. S. FERGUSON—Farm-house. 3 miles; accommodate 8. Particulars on application.

Mrs. T. HUBER—Accommodate 10. Correspondence solicited.

Mrs. G. W. HYMERS—Farm-house. 2½ miles; accommodate 8. Write for particulars.

L. M. WOODRUFF—Private cottage. Accommodate 2. Terms and full particulars on application.

Mrs. HARVEY SMITH (Bloomville Post-Office)—Will take a few city boarders for the summer. Write for particulars.

MEREDITH, DELAWARE CO.,

Is situated 2,700 feet above the sea. Has two or three churches, school, stores and shops, post-office, telephone office connecting with the telegraph lines to all important points, and semi-daily mail. This locality abounds with beautiful and extensive mountain scenery in both Delaware and Susquehanna valleys. From this elevated watchtower and "coign of vantage" we have applications for summer boarders, whose claims deserve notice.

DELHI STATION—Meredith Post-Office.

SHERMAN BISBEE—Farm-house. Accommodate 18; adults $6; rates for children on application; elevation 3,000 feet above the sea; free transportation for those remaining a few weeks; large rooms; every home comfort; convenient to post-office and telephone; semi-daily mail; good table; picturesque scenery. References on application.

I. A. PARKER—Private boarding-house. 6 miles; pleasant location; nearly 3,000 feet above the sea; no malaria or mosquitoes; convenient to churches, physician, telephone, post-office, etc.; remarkably healthy climate; pure spring water; fine views; pleasant drives; woods within easy walking distance; well-furnished rooms; table supplied with the choicest dairy products from the celebrated Meridale Farms; raise our own vegetables, poultry, etc. Terms and best references on application.

Valley of the Susquehanna.

Returning to the main line at Walton, the road climbs the hills of the divide between the waters of the Delaware and Susquehanna rivers. At the summit the road-bed is 1,800 feet above the sea.

FRANKLIN STATION, DELAWARE CO.

Four miles from Franklin Village; 1,600 feet above the sea; village of 800 inhabitants; clean, quiet, shady; fine stone walks and pleasant drives; boating and fishing in the delightful Onleout Valley; beautiful scenery; very healthful locality; has perhaps the purest water of any village in the State, from artesian wells 365 feet deep; four churches; two daily stages; telegraph and telephone lines; seat of the Delaware Literary Institute; inhabitants cultured and refined.

191 MILES FROM NEW YORK.
LOCAL, $6.10; LIMITED, $6.00;
EXCURSION, $8.80.

FRANKLIN STATION—Franklin Post-Office.

EDWARD J. COLCORD—Boarding-house. 4½ miles; accommodate 25 to 50; adults $6 and $7, according to rooms, children $3 to $5, according to age, transient $2; discount to season guests; fine large house with verandas; good views from all windows; best of water, hot and cold; first-class table; excellent sleeping arrangements; fresh country vegetables; excellent trout-fishing; good boating; first-class teams at lowest rates; good neighbors; best of society; splendid gunning; plenty of fine drives; charming scenery; free transportation; three minutes' walk from four churches; in short, a very desirable country-house. Refers to Dr. A. E. Sullard, Mr. Stephen Potter and E. P. Howe, all of Franklin, N. Y.

Mrs. CARRIE M. BARNES—Accommodate 15; adults $5. Correspondence solicited.

MATILDA B. HANFORD—Accommodate 6; adults $5 to $7. For further particulars apply as above.

Misses H. C. & S. A. BUSH—Private house. Accommodate 5; adults $5 to $7. References and full particulars on application.

Mrs. M. E. DANIELS—Accommodate 10; adults $5 to $7. Write for particulars.

FRANKLIN STATION—Croton Post-Office.

G. F. KELLOGG—Farm-house. 8 miles; accommodate 10; adults $5; house located on an elevation of 2,200 feet above tide-water; healthy climate; yard large and shady; first-class table; comfortable rooms; plenty of fresh butter, cream, milk, eggs, etc.; close to post office, telephone and church; raise own vegetables; excellent gunning and fishing. References on application.

FRANKLIN VILLAGE AND VALLEY.

SIDNEY CENTRE, DELAWARE CO.

Situated four miles from the Susquehanna river and surrounded by high and breezy hills. A number of excellent farm-houses open their hospitable doors for the reception of summer boarders.

> 103 MILES FROM NEW YORK.
> LIMITED FARE, $6.00;
> EXCURSION, $9.75.

SIDNEY CENTRE STATION—Sherruck Post-Office.

D. W. LEWIS—Small family hotel, with telephone and post-office in house, 9 miles from Sidney Centre, in the Trout Creek Valley, at the confluence of the Trout creek, the Loomis and Sherruck brooks. Hot and cold water in house; bath and sewer connections; accommodations for 12, at farm-house rates; the surroundings are unique, there being two or three miles of trout streams on property; bridle path skirting the hill-sides; pretty drives and strolls by streams and in forest; grand views. Refers to D. W. Lewis & Co., 177 Chambers Street, New York, telephone 4056 Cortlandt, New York; Postmaster, Sherruck, N. Y.

WILLIAM H. DIBBLE (Sidney Centre Post-Office)—Farm-house. ½ mile; accommodate 4; adults $5.

SIDNEY CENTRE STATION—Trout Creek Post-Office.

E. K. TEED & SON—Hotel. 5 miles; accommodate 40; adults $7 to $8, transient $2; discount to season guests; free transportation; three stories lately refitted and enlarged; centrally located in the heart of the village; grounds well shaded; good water; fine views; excellent trout-fishing in streams near by; suitable cottages and lodging-places convenient to house; good gunning; Mr. Teed is a G. A. R. man; three churches close by. References on application.

E. W. RUTENBIR (Tacoma Post-Office)—Farm-house. Accommodate 10; adults $7. Correspondence solicited.

CALVIN W. TEED (Masonville Post-Office)—Farm-house. 4 miles; accommodate 12; adults $5, children $3; free transportation; 1½ miles from lake, which is well stocked with trout, affording excellent fishing, also near forest, where first-class gunning can be had; large orchard on farm; raise own vegetables. References and full particulars on application.

SIDNEY, DELAWARE CO.

A village of 1,450 inhabitants, situated on the Susquehanna river, near its junction with the Unadilla, 999 feet above the sea. The road connects at this point in a union depot with trains of the Albany & Susquehanna Division of the Delaware & Hudson Railroad, running from Albany to Binghamton, and receives from the same Company their coal, which is run to Oswego and transferred to boats for shipment to lake ports. It is also the terminus of the branch road to Edmeston. This village has grown rapidly and more than doubled its population in six years.

> 103 MILES FROM NEW YORK.
> LOCAL, $5.45; LIMITED, $6.00;
> EXCURSION, $9.00.

SIDNEY STATION—Vallonia Springs Post-Office.

J. C. SANDS—Will take a limited number of summer boarders; adults $5 to $6. Write for particulars.

SIDNEY STATION—Bainbridge Post-Office.

G. S. GRAVES—Boarding-house. Terms and full particulars on application.

SIDNEY STATION—Oneonta Post-Office.

Miss ETHEL DOOLITTLE—Private house. Accommodate 7. Terms and particulars on application.
Mrs. R. WINTER—Would like to take a few summer boarders. Write for particulars.

SIDNEY STATION—Bennettsville Post-Office.

Mrs. H. E. UTTER—Would like to accommodate a few city boarders. Particulars furnished on application.

The New Berlin Branch.

Two and a half miles beyond Sidney the New Berlin Branch leaves the main line, and extends northward twenty-two miles along the valley of the Unadilla river, through a delightful dairy region, with its quiet, pleasant hamlets. The valley of the Unadilla is about 1,000 feet above the sea, and forms the boundary between Otsego and Chenango counties. The towns along its banks upon either side, though small, are thrifty and very prettily situated.

ROCKDALE, CHENANGO CO.

This is the first station up the branch. Here the " Uncle Zech. Curtis Spring" supplies the purest water. The drainage of the village is exceptionally good. The Unadilla river runs swiftly at this point, and a level plateau on the opposite shore, extending miles in both directions, covers with a light sandy soil all miasmatic vapors. There is a hotel with rooms " *en suite*," with plain but thoroughly good fare, at the most modest prices. There are farm-houses also that entertain summer guests, and for plain country living, without watering-place attractions, Rockdale extends a hospitable hand to all comers.

ROCKDALE STATION—Rockdale Post-Office.

C. B. MEDBURY—Farm-house. Terms, references and full particulars on application.

MT. UPTON, CHENANGO CO.

MT. UPTON STATION—Mt. Upton Post-Office.

HENRY J. HYER—Farm-house. 1 mile; open again for guests; rooms large and airy; delightful shade; picturesque scenery; within short distance of three churches; excellent hunting and fishing; boats free to guests; adults $5; first-class table; good running spring water; romantic walks and drives; healthy location; home comforts. Refers to John G. Mars, 670 Jersey Avenue, Jersey City, N. J.; Harvey Truesdel, Mt. Upton, N. Y.

HIRAM D. COLE—Private residence. Accommodate a few boarders. Particulars on application.

GILBERTSVILLE, Mt. Upton Station,

Is a thriving and beautiful village of about 700 inhabitants, three miles from Mount Upton. It has two very large and commodious hotels, which each season accommodate large numbers of city guests. The walks and drives are of the best; the fishing is also excellent.

LIMITED FARE, $5.21; EXCURSION, $9.00.

MT. UPTON STATION—Gilbertsville Post-Office.

L. S. ROCKWELL—Farm-house. 7 miles; accommodate 10; adults $5, children reduction; large comfortable house, cool in the hottest weather; delightful location; fruit, milk and cream in abundance; raise our own vegetables. References on application.

Mrs. R. B. MYRICK—Desires boarders for the summer. Terms and particulars on application.

SOUTH NEW BERLIN.

LIMITED FARE, $5.48. EXCURSION, $9.00.

NEW BERLIN, Chenango Co.,

Has a population of about 1,200, with four churches and an academy. It is a busy village, surrounded by high and breezy hills. The country is exceedingly rich and fertile. Silver Lake, beautifully situated one mile from the village, affords a fine rendezvous for picnic parties. The Unadilla river is well stocked with black bass, pickerel, perch, and an occasional trout. The hotels in the village are excellent, and give ample accommodation at reasonable rates.

227 MILES FROM NEW YORK. LIMITED FARE, $5.70; EXCURSION, $9.00.

EDMESTON, Otsego Co.

Edmeston is a picturesque village of nearly 600 inhabitants, located at the terminus of the New Berlin Branch of the Ontario & Western Railway. A rich farming community surrounds it, and butter, cheese and milk are its chief exports. It is the principal village in the Wharton Valley, and consequently a trade centre for the eight or ten smaller villages that nestle about it within a radius of ten miles. The Wharton creek flows southerly through the valley and village, and furnishes never-failing water-power. As to climate, there is no more healthful spot on the footstool. Since the advent of the railroad it has become quite a resort for city people, who find ample accommodations at the three large hotels in the place, and at farm residences. The increase in population the past year has been over one hundred, and some twelve or fifteen new buildings have been erected.

234 MILES FROM NEW YORK. LIMITED FARE, $5.91; EXCURSION, $9.00.

Along the Chenango.

GUILFORD, CHENANGO CO.

| LOCAL, $5.70; LIMITED, $6.00; EXCURSION, $9.00. |

Returning to the main line, we commence another ascending grade over the divide between the Susquehanna and its largest tributary, the Chenango. The village of Guilford is surrounded by a rich agricultural district. Has many pleasant summer abiding-places. The fishing is excellent, as the people of the village take considerable interest in the fish laws, and protect the many lakes in their vicinity by game laws, as well as stocking them with lake trout, and the brooks with brook trout.

GUILFORD STATION—Guilford Post-Office.

Miss JENNIE NORTH—Farm-house. 1 mile; accommodate 10; adults $5; the farm consists of 100 acres, and has a large lake affording excellent bass and pickerel fishing; boats and fishing-tackle free to guests; good gunning; first-class livery attached. References from former guests on application.

OXFORD, CHENANGO CO.

| 216 MILES FROM NEW YORK. LOCAL, $5.60; LIMITED, $6.00; EXCURSION, $9.00. |

Oxford is one of the prettiest villages in central New York. It is situated on both banks of the Chenango river, 1,156 feet above the sea. It has a healthy location and ample drainage. By the last census the village has a population of 1,630, a gain of 444 in ten years, and also shows the largest gain in per cent. of any town in the county. It is well laid out, has fine parks and clean, shaded streets, and is supplied with pure spring water from the surrounding hills. As a resort for summer boarders it is rapidly gaining in popular favor, and last season accommodated a large number. There are three hotels and several private boarding-houses—one in particular, an old family mansion with the finest surroundings in town—that solicit summer boarders.

The heathfulness of the town, its society and advantages, beautiful drives, etc., are not to be compared with any town of its size. There are six churches, bank, telegraph offices, and numerous well-conducted business places, also an opera-house on the ground-floor that presents many first-class entertainments. The Academy, one of

CROSSING THE DELAWARE.

the oldest in the State, founded in 1794 and in successful operation ever since, is now one of the best-conducted schools in the State. There are several manufactories in operation in the place, a chair factory and a basket factory being among the largest, but the chief industry of the town is its quarries of excellent blue-stone.

OXFORD STATION—Oxford Post-Office.

ST. JAMES HOTEL—Located in centre of town; accommodate 25; 30 rooms; adults $6 to $10, children $2 to $5, transient $1.50 to $2; discount to season guests; 'bus meets all trains; has broad and commodious verandas, with a lawn surrounding; profusion of shade; faces the public square, which contains fountain; pure spring water; raise our own vegetables; good fishing and boating in Chenango river and the many ponds in the vicinity; first-class livery; upon the whole, a delightful summer home. References on application.

OXFORD STATION—McDonough Post-Office.

CHARLES LEWIS—Town residence. 10 miles; accommodate 10; adults $4.50, children $3.50, transient 75 cents; discount to season guests; raise own vegetables; suitable cottages and lodging-places near house; good fishing and gunning; boats and fishing-tackle free; first-class table; home comforts; high ceilings; running water; three churches near by; free transportation; pleasant walks and drives. Refers to C. W. Babcock, Middlefield, N. Y. Correspondence solicited.

NORWICH, CHENANGO CO.

The county seat of Chenango County, 1,100 feet above the sea. It is a remarkably clean and well-built town, with splendid water-works. Its streets are wide and amply shaded, its walks well paved. The county buildings do credit to the county, and its public squares are an ornament to the place. It has seven churches of as many different denominations, two banks and two newspaper offices. It is largely engaged in the manufacture of hammers and other hardware, pianos, carriages, sashes and blinds, etc. Its population is about 5,000. It is a favorite resort for summer visitors, and few places can be found where the heat of our city summers can be more surely and delightfully escaped.

227 MILES FROM NEW YORK. LOCAL, $6.15; LIMITED, $6.00; EXCURSION, $9.00.

EARLVILLE, MADISON CO.

This is a place of 1,000 inhabitants; is situated on a slight elevation in the beautiful and broad Chenango Valley; has three new and modern hotels; the streets are lined on either side with elegant maples; the buildings are nearly all new, fire having destroyed the place in 1886; three new and elegant churches; national bank; seven mails received and seven sent out daily; several trains daily to New York, Syracuse, Oswego and Utica direct; numerous ponds and streams, including pretty Lake

240 MILES FROM NEW YORK. LIMITED FARE, $6.00; EXCURSION, $10.00.

Earlville, near by, in which the most desirable varieties of fish are plentiful; fine forests and good hunting; purest of water throughout the town and perfect drainage. Earlville is pronounced the most thriving and beautiful place in central New York.

EARLVILLE STATION—Earlville Post-Office.
H. B. Kinney—Hotel. Accommodate 40; adults $5, children $3.

EARLVILLE STATION—Poolville Post-Office.
Dr. C. D. Green—Everett House. Rates, references and full particulars on application.

EARLVILLE STATION—Cazenovia Post-Office.
F. C. Murtaugh—Hotel. Accommodate 75; adults $12.

Utica Division.

Extending from Randallsville to Utica, a distance of thirty-one miles, with a branch from Clinton to Rome of twelve miles. Throughout the entire distance the line runs through a beautiful country devoted largely to the cultivation of hops.

HAMILTON, Madison Co.

The first station is a wealthy village of some 2,000 inhabitants, with broad, shady, well-kept streets. It has two good hotels. The Madison University, Hamilton Theological Seminary and Colgate Academy are located here. These three distinct institutions of learning are under the care of the corporation of Madison University. The present number of students in attendance is about 325.

247 MILES FROM NEW YORK.
LOCAL, $6.61; LIMITED, $8.00;
EXCURSION, $10.00.

Peeksport, Bouckville, Solsville and Deansville are small, thriving villages, surrounded with broad, fertile hop-fields.

HAMILTON STATION—Hamilton Post-Office.
A. M. Sawdey—1 mile; accommodate 10; adults $3. Particulars on application.

ORISKANY FALLS, Oneida Co.

A thriving village of about 800 inhabitants. Midway between the junction with the main line and the city of Utica. It has four churches and graded school. Woolen manufacture is an important industry. Surrounding farm lands devoted to dairying and hop-growing. Surface hilly and

257 MILES FROM NEW YORK.
LIMITED FARE, $8.00;
EXCURSION, $10.00.

scenery romantic. Has two well-kept hotels and a valuable mineral spring.

ORISKANY FALLS STATION—Oriskany Post-Office.

Mrs. A. E. SARGENT—Hotel. ¼ mile; accommodate 15; adults $7.
P. J. HORTON—Hotel. ¼ mile; accommodate 4; adults $7.

ORIKANY FALLS STATION—Babcock Hill Post-Office.

Mrs. R. C. MILLER—Accommodate 5; adults $5. Full particulars on application.

SOLSVILLE STATION—Solsville Post-Office.

R. A. GOODRICH—Boarding-house. 1 mile; accommodate 6; adults $6 to $7. Write for particulars.

DEANSVILLE STATION—Deansville Post-Office.

Mrs. WM. CURRIE—Farm-house. Ten minutes' walk; accommodate 8; adults $4, children $3, transient 75 cents; five minutes' walk to church; ½ mile of private road on farm; picturesque scenery; comfortable rooms; healthy location; first-class table; good livery attached. Refers to Dr. Claude Wilson, Waterville, N. Y., and Dr. James I. Scollard, Clinton, N. Y.

CLINTON, ONEIDA CO.

"The village of schools," population about 2,500. One of the most charming villages in New York State, noted for its beautiful situation and healthful surroundings. The seat of Hamilton College and the Litchfield Observatory; two seminaries for young ladies, Houghton and Cottage, and two boarding-schools for boys, Clinton Grammar School and Kirkland Hall, have given the village a wide reputation as an educational centre. Near the village are the smelting-furnaces of the Franklin Iron Manufacturing Company and the Kirkland Iron Company, and also the extensive iron-ore mines of the former Company. Various other manufacturing industries give the town a business-like aspect, which is very pleasing in connection with its literary and scholastic tendencies. Immediately south of the village are located three mineral springs, whose waters are fast gaining a wide reputation and sale for their medicinal properties. Clinton is in the midst of the hop-producing region, and is one of the leading hop-markets of the State. The substantial and comfortable homes of the well-to-do farming community offer delightful opportunities for summer boarders, who enjoy wholesome living amid the quiet peace of rural scenes. Nine miles from Utica (population 40,000) and twelve miles from Rome (population 15,000).

[267 MILES FROM NEW YORK. LOCAL, $7.36; LIMITED, $8.00; EXCURSION, $10.00.]

UTICA, ONEIDA CO.

One of the most enterprising cities of central New York, with 40,000 inhabitants. It is largely engaged in the manufacture of boots and shoes, clothing, cotton and woolen goods. Next to Rochester it is the largest manufacturer of clothing in this country. Five railroads reach Utica.

[276 MILES FROM NEW YORK. LOCAL, $7.42; LIMITED, $8.00; EXCURSION, $10.00.]

ROME, Oneida Co.,

Is a city of 15,000 inhabitants, lying in the beautiful Mohawk Valley.

> 250 MILES FROM NEW YORK.
> LOCAL, $7.77; LIMITED, $8.30;
> EXCURSION, $10.00.

The city is largely devoted to manufacturing: the Rome Locomotive Works, Brass and Copper Mills, Rome Merchant Iron Mill, saddlery, sash, blind and knitting factories being among the most important. Is the eastern terminus of the Rome, Watertown & Ogdensburg Railroad. The sweet-corn canning industry in this locality takes the lead in this country. Rome is one of the most beautiful and healthful places in central New York. With broad, well-shaded streets, and flagged sidewalks, it commands the admiration of all visitors. There are beautiful locations for country-seats near the city. The Central New York School for Deaf-Mutes is located here, and is well worth a visit. It has new buildings at a cost of $150,000. Hotel accommodations are good at moderate rates. Many trout-fishing and camping parties make this point their headquarters during the season.

ROME STATION—Rome Post-Office.

Mrs. Frank Midlan—Accommodate 6. Full information on application.

ROME STATION—Florence Post-Office.

John Crego—Farm-house. Accommodate 8; adults $7. Write for particulars.

Through the Hop Country.

EATON, MADISON CO.

An enterprising little village of 500 inhabitants, lying in the valley,

> 249 MILES FROM NEW YORK.
> LIMITED FARE, $5.60;
> EXCURSION, $10.00.

surrounded with broad hop-fields and hospitable farm-houses.

MORRISVILLE, MADISON CO.

Fifteen miles from Oneida; county seat; population 900; high

> LIMITED FARE, $5.60;
> EXCURSION, $10.00.

elevation; village two miles from Ontario & Western Railway; fine hunting and fishing in vicinity. Three large hotels and several private boarding-houses. The village is beautifully laid out with wide, well-kept streets lined with large maples. Principal industry, manufacturing of cutters. This place during the past ten years has become quite a popular resort for New York summer boarders. The principal agricultural industry in this vicinity is the raising of hops, which is carried on to a great extent.

MORRISVILLE STATION—Morrisville Post-Office.

J. H. WESTCOTT—Farm-house. 4 miles; accommodate 6. Terms on application.

PRATT'S, MADISON CO.

Largely devoted to the cultivation of hops. Has numerous

> 264 MILES FROM NEW YORK.
> LIMITED FARE, $5.60;
> EXCURSION, $10.00.

fine trout streams in its vicinity, furnishing excellent and unlimited enjoyment to the lovers of reel and rod.

PRATT'S STATION—Pratt's Hollow Post-Office.

G. H. LEWIS—Hotel. ¼ mile; accommodate 10; adults $8, transient $1.50.

L. M. LYNCH—Farm-house. ¼ mile; accommodate 4; adults $8, children $5, transient $1.50.

KENWOOD, MADISON CO.

At this point is located the "Oneida Community, Limited,"

> 264 MILES FROM NEW YORK.
> LOCAL, $7.32; LIMITED, $6.60;
> EXCURSION, $10.00.

consisting of over 300 members, with a fine estate of 650 acres, beautifully situated, and under the most admirable cultivation; a commodious mansion, and several mills and manufactories. Their reorganization, in 1880, has

removed whatever was objectionable in their past management, and they have entered upon a new career as a business organization under the most favorable circumstances. They are engaged in the manufacture of hunters' traps and satchels, and the preparation of canned vegetables and fruits. All their manufactures have gained an enviable reputation for excellence.

ONEIDA, MADISON CO.

Connections are made here with the New York Central R.R. The village contains a population of 6,020, has a fine system of water-works, and is lit with electric lights. There are two good graded schools, eight churches, five banks, two semi-weekly and two weekly newspapers. The Chappell, Chase, Maxwell & Co.'s Casket-manufactory, a spring-bed factory, chuck-works, wagon-works, knitting-mill, cigar-manufactories, and other manufactures give employment to 1,200 hands, making a thriving and rapidly growing village. After leaving Oneida, the topography of the country undergoes a change. Instead of a hilly country, with its succession of gracefully rounded summits and deep secluded valleys, we find a level, rolling surface, resembling somewhat the prairies of the West.

SYLVAN BEACH, ONEIDA CO.

Beautifully situated on the point of land lying between Oneida Lake on the north and Wood river on the south. Its great natural beauty has made it the favorite resort of Utica, Rome, Oneida and Syracuse people, many of whom have erected cottages in which the entire summer season is spent. The bathing is unequaled by any inland summer resort; the beach of white sand gently declines for a half-mile before the water reaches a dangerous depth, and extends for miles around the lake, forming an inland Coney Island—perfectly safe for children. Bathing-suits and attendants may be had at reasonable rates at the bathing-houses. Boats, oarsmen and fishing-tackle may be had at the dock. Bass, pickerel, pike, perch, and other fish are abundant in both the river and lake. The wild shores of the lake and the neighboring islands afford good duck, woodcock, partridge and snipe shooting in season. This is the largest and one of the most beautiful of the inland lakes of New York, being twenty-seven miles long by seven wide, and has an area of about 57,000 acres. Its surface is 369 feet above the sea, and 142½ above Lake Ontario. It occupies a portion of four counties, viz.: Oneida, Oswego, Madison and Onondaga. Its outlet is the Oneida river which, after flowing westward for eighteen miles, unites with the Seneca river to form the Oswego. The lake contains

*270 MILES FROM NEW YORK.
LIMITED FARE, $6.77;
EXCURSION, $10.00.*

ALGONQUIN HOTEL.
(Sylvan Beach.)

two islands (Frenchman's and Lotus), and there probably cannot be found two more healthful spots in the State. It is said of these islands that, "when the Great Spirit formed the world, His smile rested on the waters of the blue Oneida, and Frenchman's Island arose to greet it. He laughed, and Lotus Island came up to listen." On Frenchman's Island is located the Sylvan House, which is reached from Cleveland or Constantia (being four miles from the latter place) by steam-yacht. The salubrity of climate, cool breezes, great fertility of soil, bathing, boating, fishing, and an absolute freedom from the restraints of fashion render this a delightful summer retreat.

NORTH BAY, ONEIDA CO.

LIMITED FARE, $5.00. EXCURSION, $10.00.

NORTH BAY STATION—North Bay Post-Office.

GEORGE E. BUTLER—Hotel. Close to station; accommodate 40; adults $7, children $4, transient $1.50; hotel has 500 feet of piazza; pure spring water; no mosquitoes or malaria; boats and bathing-houses free to guests. References on application.

WEST VIENNA STATION—West Vienna Post-Office.

Mrs. E. JEWELL—Hotel. At station; accommodate 15; adults $5 to $10, children according to age, transient $1.

CLEVELAND, OSWEGO CO.

LIMITED FARE, $6.07; EXCURSION, $10.00.

Pleasantly located on the north shore of Oneida Lake, with a population of about 870. The people hospitable, enterprising and liberal. The village is surrounded with excellent roads, and embraces among its attractions two delightful groves on the lake-shore, which are resorted to on moonlight nights by dancing parties from across the lake. Cleveland has two large factories for the manufacture of window-glass; has four churches and three hotels; row and sail boats for pleasure or fishing parties can be obtained; splendid bass and pike fishing.

BERNHARD'S BAY, OSWEGO CO.

LIMITED FARE, $6.16. EXCURSION, $10.00.

On the lake, with large glass-works.

CONSTANTIA, OSWEGO CO.

LIMITED FARE, $6.25. EXCURSION, $10.00.

The nearest point to Frenchman's Island in Oneida Lake. The village is pleasantly located on the lake-shore.

WEST MONROE, Oswego Co.

LIMITED FARE, $6.37.   EXCURSION, $10.00.

CENTRAL SQUARE, Oswego Co.

The road crosses at this point the Syracuse Division of the Rome, Watertown & Ogdensburg Railroad, and connection is made for the Thousand Islands via the Rome, Watertown & Ogdensburg Railroad to Cape Vincent and the steamer *St. Lawrence*.

> 300 MILES FROM NEW YORK.
> LOCAL, $7.75; LIMITED, $8.80;
> EXCURSION, $10.00.

FULTON, Oswego Co.

It is situated at the Falls of the Oswego river, and has one of the best water-powers in the State, having a fall of twenty-five feet in less than half a mile, with the great and unfailing volume of water supplied by the Oswego river and its feeders. The water-power is utilized by five large flouring-mills, foundries, machine-shops, knife-works, two paper-mills, planing-mills, plaster-mills, etc. On the west side of the river, and supplied by the same falls, are the great "Worsted Mills" of the Oswego Falls Manufacturing Company, said to be the largest manufactory of worsted goods in the United States. These mills run over 14,000 spindles and over 600 looms, use 35,000 to 40,000 pounds of wool weekly, and employ nearly 1,000 operatives. The village has seven churches, two national banks, one savings-bank, two newspaper offices, and five public schools of high reputation. Here is situated, also, Falley Seminary, long known as one of the best educational institutions of its class in the State. The population of Fulton, including Oswego Falls, on the main bank of the river, immediately opposite and connected with it by two iron bridges, was about 6,000 in 1880.

> 313 MILES FROM NEW YORK.
> LOCAL, $7.75; LIMITED, $8.80;
> EXCURSION, $10.00.

FULTON STATION—Fulton Post-Office.
L. R. CAFFREY—Clark House. Adults $2. Write for particulars.

Lake Ontario.

OSWEGO, Oswego Co.

Oswego, the northern lake terminus of the road, is a very attractive city. The streets are broad and shaded; the blocks are 200 to 400 feet. There are two large parks and several of lesser size. It has many fine public buildings, among which the most notable are: The Custom-house and Post-office, built by the National Government; the City Hall; the State Normal and Training School; the State Armory; the Gerritt Smith Library; the Home for the Homeless; the Orphan Asylum; the High School, and the Academy of Music. Several of the hotels and business warehouses are fine massive buildings of very tasteful architecture. The Doolittle House, in particular, is—in its architecture, the perfection of its appointments, its extent and its admirable management—a house which will compare favorably with the great hotels of our largest cities. The Deep Rock Mineral Springs, which have achieved a good reputation in rheumatic and kidney diseases, are on the premises, and their waters are furnished free to the guests of the house. There are sulphur springs of acknowledged virtue in the same vicinity. Oswego has many claims to the attention of the tourist and pleasure-seeker. It is beautifully situated, facing Lake Ontario on its northwest front, and from the bold bluffs or escarpments along the lake commands a view of the distant Canada shore and of the St. Lawrence, which, over rapids and through a wilderness of islands, carries the waters of the lake on toward the sea; its extensive falls and slack-water navigation, which add beauty as well as wealth to the city; its unrivaled facilities for pleasurable navigation, whether in stately steamer, white-winged yacht or steam launch; its inexhaustable resources for the sportsmen of every degree in its trout streams, its black-bass fishing, its lake fishing, where muskallonge, white-fish, salmon trout, land-locked salmon, and now the finest sea-salmon, pike, sturgeon and other "monsters of the bubbling deep" contend for the honor of being caught.

OSWEGO STATION—Oswego Post-Office.

DANIEL PERRY—Farm-house. 3 miles; accommodate 9; adults $5 to $6, children $2 to $4, transient $1; convenient to Niagara Falls and Thousand Islands; sea-shore and fine inland scenery combined; lovely drives; good bathing and fishing; first-class board on fruit farm; raise own vegetables. Refers to Mrs. Frank Bowman, 345 9th Street, South Brooklyn, N. Y., and Mrs. A. D. Moore, 1060 DeKalb Avenue, Brooklyn, N. Y.

FOR SALE OR TO RENT—A magnificent cottage, house and barn, with one acre of land, modern improvements, water, electric light, etc., situated on the west bank of the Oswego river, ten minutes' drive from the Oswego City Hall, post-office, depots and steamboat docks. Address W. J. Bulger, Oswego, N. Y.

E. E. ROOT—Lake Shore House. Accommodate 150; adults $7 to $10, children half.

OSWEGO STATION—Fruit Valley Post-Office.

Mrs. E. CORNING LAMB—Farm-house. 3 miles; 6 sleeping-rooms; accommodate 6 to 8; adults $5, children half, transient $1; free transportation; have a good house and pleasant grounds, near Lake Ontario, with boats to let on the beach; fine grove well fitted up for parties; a pleasant and agreeable place to spend the summer; raise own vegetables; plenty of fruit; good gunning and fishing. Refers to C. H. Buttler, Druggist, Oswego, N. Y., and Samuel Burchard, Oswego, N.Y.

OSWEGO STATION—Port Ontario Post-Office.

Mrs. C. F. RUSSELL—Farm-house. 3 miles; accommodate 8; adults $6, children $4, transient 75 cents.

OSWEGO STATION—Mexico Post-Office.

J. C. DARLING—Will rent a furnished cottage at Thousand Island Park, N. Y. For particulars apply as above.

The Circular or Card of any Hotel or Boarding-house mentioned in this book may be obtained without charge from the Recreation Department of The Christian Union, Clinton Hall, Astor Place, New York City.

Summer Excursion Routes.

THE following Routes have been arranged, and Tickets may be procured from any Ticket Agent of this Company in New York, Brooklyn, or Hoboken, or at the General Passenger Office, 56 Beaver Street, New York.

Tickets will be on sale from June 1st to September 30th, and will be valid for return passage up to and including November 1st, 1892, and will permit stop-over at pleasure of passenger.

Other routes will be arranged at correspondingly low rates upon application to Agents or to the General Passenger Agent.

NIAGARA FALLS, BUFFALO, Etc.

Exc. No. 1, Form 360—NIAGARA FALLS and Return.
New York, Ont. & West'n R'y......to Oswego
Rome, Water'n & Ogd'g R.R..to Niagara Falls
Returning via same route.
Rate from New York..............$15 00

Exc. No. 2, Form 250—NIAGARA FALLS and Return.
New York, Ont. & West'n R'y to Oneida Castle
West Shore R.R.............. to Niagara Falls
Returning via same route.
Rate from New York..............$16 00

Exc. No. 3, Form 19—BUFFALO and Return.
ROUTE GOING :
New York, Ont. & West'n R'y......to Oswego
Rome, Water'n & Ogd'g R.R..to Niagara Falls
N. Y. C. & H. R.R.................. to Buffalo
ROUTE RETURNING :
West Shore R.R............to Oneida Castle
New York, Ont. & West'n R'y...to New York
Rate from New York..............$15 50

Exc. No. 4, Form 359—BUFFALO, N. Y., and Return.
New York, Ont. & West'n R'y to Oneida Castle
West Shore R.R............. ....to Buffalo
Returning via same route.
Rate from New York $16 00

MONTREAL, QUEBEC, Etc.

Exc. No. 5, Form 248—MONTREAL and Return.
ROUTE GOING:
New York, Ont. & West'n R'y to Central Square
Rome, Water'n & Ogd'g R.R..to Cape Vincent
Steamer " St. Lawrence"... to Alexandria Bay
Richelieu & Ontario Nav. Co.......to Montreal
ROUTE RETURNING:
Grand Trunk R'y... ....to Rouse's Point
Delaware & Hud. Canal Co's R.R ..to Saratoga
Delaware & Hud. Canal Co's R.R....to Albany
Day Line Steamers................to New York
Rate from New York..............$23 10

Exc. No. 6, Form 247—MONTREAL and Return.
ROUTE GOING:
New York, Ont. & West'n R'y to Central Square
Rome, Watert'n & Ogd'g R.R. to Cape Vincent
Steamer "St. Lawrence".....to Alexandria Bay
Richelieu & Ontario Nav. Co......to Montreal
ROUTE RETURNING:
Grand Trunk R'y............to Rouse's Point
Delaware & Hud. Canal Co's R.R..to Saratoga
Delaware & Hud. Canal Co's R.R....to Albany
West Shore R.R.................to New York
Rate from New York..............$23 50

Exc. No. 7, Form 249—MONTREAL and Return.
ROUTE GOING:
New York, Ont. & West'n R'y to Central Square
Rome, Water'n & Ogd'g R.R...to Cape Vincent
Steamer "St. Lawrence" . to Alexandria Bay
Richelieu & Ontario Nav. Co......to Montreal

SUMMER EXCURSION ROUTES.

ROUTE RETURNING:
Grand Trunk R'y .... to Rouse's Point
Delaware & Hud. Canal Co's R.R. to Plattsburg
Champlain Trans. Co........ to Ft. Ticonderoga
Delaware & Hud. Canal Co's R.R...to Baldwin
Lake George Steamer .... to Caldwell
Delaware & Hud. Canal Co's R.R.. to Saratoga
Delaware & Hud. Canal Co's R.R.... to Albany
West Shore R.R................... to New York

Rate from New York $25 00

Exc. No. 8, Form 29—MONTREAL and Return.

New York, Ont. & West'n R'y to Central Square
Rome, Water'n & Ogd'g R.R.. to Cape Vincent
Steamer "St. Lawrence"....to Alexandria Bay
Richelieu & Ontario Nav. Co........to Montreal

Returning via same route.

Rate from New York................ $23 75

Exc. No. 9, Form 35—MONTREAL and Return.

ROUTE GOING:
New York, Ont. & West'n R'y to Central Square
Rome, Water'n & Ogd'g R.R.. to Cape Vincent
Steamer "St. Lawrence"....to Alexandria Bay
Richelieu & Ontario Nav. Co........to Montreal

ROUTE RETURNING:
Richelieu & Ontario Nav. Co. to Alexandria Bay
Steamer "St. Lawrence"......to Cape Vincent
Rome, Water'n & Ogd'g R.R... to Niagara Falls
West Shore R.R............... to Oneida Castle
New York, Ont. & West'n R'y....to New York

Rate from New York................ $33 10

Exc. No. 10, Form 46—MONTREAL and Return.

ROUTE GOING:
New York, Ont. & West'n R'y to Central Square
Rome, Water'n & Ogd'g R.R.. to Cape Vincent
Steamer "St. Lawrence"....to Alexandria Bay
Richelieu & Ontario Nav. Co......to Montreal

ROUTE RETURNING:
Grand Trunk R'y.................. to St. Johns
Central Vermont R.R.. to White River Junction
Boston & Maine R.R......... .....to Concord
Concord & Montreal R.R........... to Nashua
Boston & Maine R.R................. to Boston
Sound Steamers................... to New York

Rate from New York................ $26 50

Exc. No. 11, Form A-43—MONTREAL and Return.

ROUTE GOING:
New York, Ont. & West'n R'y to Central Square
Rome, Water'n & Ogd'g R.R.. to Cape Vincent
Steamer "St. Lawrence"....to Alexandria Bay
Richelieu & Ontario Nav. Co.......to Montreal

ROUTE RETURNING:
Canadian Pacific R'y............... to Newport
Boston & Maine R.R.........to St. Johnsbury
Boston & Maine R.R .... to Fabyans
Boston & Maine R.R....to Bethlehem Junction
Boston & Maine R.R............... to Concord
Concord & Montreal R.R............to Nashua
Boston & Maine R.R................to Boston
Sound Steamers ....to New York

Rate from New York............... $26 50

Exc. No. 12, Form 350—MONTREAL, QUEBEC and Return.

ROUTE GOING:
New York, Ont. & West'n R'y to Central Square
Rome, Water'n & Ogd'g R.R.. to Cape Vincent
Steamer "St. Lawrence"....to Alexandria Bay
Richelieu & Ontario Nav. Co.......to Montreal
G. T. R'y or Rich. & Ont. Nav. Co... to Quebec
Rich. & Ont. Nav. Co.......... to Ha-Ha Bay

ROUTE RETURNING:
Rich. & Ont. Nav. Co................to Quebec
Quebec Central R.R.............to Sherbrook
Boston & Maine R.R .. to Newport & Wells River
Boston & Maine R.R .... to Concord
Concord & Montreal R.R............to Nashua
Boston & Maine R.R................to Boston
Sound Steamers....................to New York

Rate from New York.......... .....$30 50

Single Trip Tickets to Montreal.

Exc. No. 13, Form 465—MONTREAL.

New York, Ont. & West'n R'y...... to Oswego
Rome, Water'n & Ogd'g R.R..to Massena Sp'gs
Grand Trunk R'y.................. to Montreal

Rate from New York $10 00

Exc. No. 14, Form 548—MONTREAL, via NIAGARA FALLS.

New York, Ont. & West'n R'y...... to Oswego
Rome, Water'n & Ogd'g R.R..to Niagara Falls
Grand Trunk R'y .... to Pt. Dalhousie
Steamer "Empress of India "....... to Toronto
Rich. & Ont. Nav. Co. or G'd T. R'y to Kingston
Rich. & Ont. Nav. Co. or G'd T. R'y to Montreal

Rate from New York...... ....$19 00

SUMMER EXCURSION ROUTES.

Exc. No. 15 Form 293—MONTREAL.

New York, Ont. & West'n R'y to Central Square
Rome, Water'n & Ogd'g R.R...to Ogdensburg
Ferry..............................to Prescott
Grand Trunk R'y.................to Montreal
    Rate from New York................$10 00

Exc. No. 16—CHICOUTIMI, and the SAGUENAY RIVER.

Rich. & Ont. Nav. Co. from Quebec to
Murray Bay and return....................$4 00
Tadousac and return...................... 5 00
Ha-Ha Bay and return.................... 8 00
Chicoutimi and return.................... 8 00

Routes Returning from Montreal.

(To be issued only in connection with tickets sold to Montreal.)

Exc. No. 17—MONTREAL to NEW YORK.

Grand Trunk R'y...................to St. Johns
Central Vermont R.R.........to Bellows Falls
Cheshire R.R......................to Fitchburg
Fitchburg R.R........................to Boston
Sound Steamers...................to New York
    Rate from Montreal.................$13 50

Exc. No. 18—MONTREAL to NEW YORK.

Grand Trunk R'y....................to Portland
Boston & Maine R.R..............to Boston
Sound Line Steamers..............to New York
    Rate from Montreal.................$13 50

Exc. No. 19—MONTREAL to NEW YORK.

Grand Trunk R'y ....to Rouse's Point
Delaware & Hud. Canal Co's R.R..to Plattsburg
Lake Champlain Steamer... to Ft. Ticonderoga
Delaware & Hud. Canal Co's R.R...to Saratoga
Delaware & Hud. Canal Co's R.R...to Albany
West Shore R.R..................to New York
    Rate from Montreal $11 50

Exc. No. 20—MONTREAL to NEW YORK.

Grand Trunk R'y...................to St. Johns
Central Vermont R.R..to White River Junction
Boston & Maine R.R ....to Concord
Boston & Maine R.R ....to Boston
Sound Line Steamers............to New York
    Rate from Montreal $13 50

Exc. No. 21—MONTREAL to NEW YORK.

Grand Trunk R'y............ to Rouse's Point
Delaware & Hud.Canal Co's R.R..to Plattsburg
Champlain Trans. Co.......to Ft. Ticonderoga
Delaware & Hud. Canal Co's R.R...to Baldwin
Lake George Steamer...............to Caldwell
Delaware & Hud. Canal Co's R.R...to Saratoga
Fitchburg R.R........................to Boston
Sound Line Steamers..... ....to New York
    Rate from Montreal..................17 15

Exc. No. 22—MONTREAL to NEW YORK.

Canadian Pacific R'y ....to Newport
Boston & Maine R.R...........to Wells River
Boston & Maine R.R.................to Concord
Boston & Maine R.R.................to Boston
Sound Line Steamers............ to New York
    Rate from Montreal................$13 50

Exc. No. 23—MONTREAL to NEW YORK.

Grand Trunk R'y............ to Rouse's Point
Delaware & Hud. Canal Co's R.R...to Albany
Hudson River Day Line Steamer..to New York
    Rate from Montreal..................$9 60

Same route to Albany, thence People's Line (night steamers) rate from Montreal, $8 95

Exc. No. 24—MONTREAL to NEW YORK.

Grand Trunk R'y............ to Rouse's Point
Delaware & Hud. Canal Co's R.R..to Plattsburg
Champlain Trans. Co............. to Burlington
Central Vermont R.R............to Montpelier
Montpelier & Wells River R.R..to Wells River
Boston & Maine R,R.................to Concord
Boston & Maine R.R.................to Boston
Sound Line Steamers............ to New York
    Rate from Montreal.................$13 50

Exc. No. 25—MONTREAL to NEW YORK.

Canadian Pacific R'y............. to Newport
Boston & Maine R.R......... .to Wells River
Boston & Maine R.R................to Fabyans
Maine Central R.R......... to North Conway
Boston & Maine R.R..................to Boston
Sound Line Steamers............ to New York
    Rate from Montreal................$13 50

SUMMER EXCURSION ROUTES.

Exc. No. 26—MONTREAL to NEW YORK.

Canadian Pacific R'y .... to Newport
Boston & Maine R.R ..... to White River Junc.
Central Vermont R.R .... to Windsor
Vermont Valley R.R .... to Brattleboro
Central Vermont R.R .... to South Vernon
Connecticut River R.R .... to Springfield
N. Y., N. H. & Hartford R.R .... to New York
Rate from Montreal $10 00

Exc. No. 27—MONTREAL to NEW YORK.

Canadian Pacific R'y .... to Newport
Boston & Maine R.R .... to St. Johnsbury
St. Johnsb'y & Lake Champlain R.R. to Scott's
Boston & Maine R.R .... to Fabyans
Maine Central R.R .... to Crawford House
Maine Central R.R .... to North Conway
Boston & Maine R.R .... to Boston
Old Colony R.R .... to Fall River
Fall River Line Steamers.......... to New York
Rate from Montreal $13 50

Exc. No. 28—MONTREAL to NEW YORK.

Grand Trunk R'y.................... to St. Johns
Central Vermont R.R .... to Windsor
Vermont Valley R.R .... to Brattleboro
Central Vermont R.R .... to Miller's Falls
New London & Northern R.R .. to New London
Norwich & Worcester Line St'rs ... to New York
Rate from Montreal $10 00

Exc. No. 29—MONTREAL to NEW YORK.

Canadian Pacific R'y .... to Newport
Boston & Maine R.R .... to St. Johnsbury
Boston & Maine R.R .... to Lunenburg
Portland & Ogdensburg R.R .... to Fabyans
Boston & Maine R.R ...... to Bethlehem Junc.
Boston & Maine R.R .... to Concord
Concord & Montreal R.R .... to Nashua
Boston & Maine R.R .... to Boston
Old Colony R.R .... to Fall River
Fall River Line Steamers.......... to New York
Rate from Montreal $13 50

Exc. No. 30—MONTREAL to NEW YORK.

Canadian Pacific R'y .... to Newport
Boston & Maine R.R .... to St. Johnsbury
Maine Central R.R .... to Lunenburg
Maine Central R.R .... to Fabyans

Concord & Montreal R.R ... to Base Mt. Wash'n
Mt. Washington R.R .... to Summit
Stage (9 miles)................... to Glen House
Stage (14 miles)................. to Glen Station
Maine Central R.R .... to North Conway
Boston & Maine R.R .... to Boston
Old Colony R.R .... to Fall River
Fall River Line Steamers.......... to New York
Rate from Montreal $25 00

THOUSAND ISLANDS, ALEXANDRIA BAY, Etc.

Exc. No. 31, Form 30—ALEXANDRIA BAY and Return.

ROUTE GOING:

New York, Ont. & West'n R'y.to Central Square
Rome, Watert'n & Ogd'g R.R.. to Cape Vincent
Steamer "St. Lawrence".... to Alexandria Bay

ROUTE RETURNING:

Steamer "St. Lawrence"...... to Cape Vincent
Rome, Water'n & Ogd'g R.R... to Niagara Falls
West Shore R.R .... to Oneida Castle
New York, Ont. & West'n R'y.... to New York
Rate from New York $23 60

Exc. No. 32, Form 335—THOUSAND ISLANDS and GEORGIAN BAY. Returning via Toronto and Niagara Falls.

ROUTE GOING:

New York, Ont. & West'n R'y.to Central Square
Rome, Water'n & Ogd'g R.R... to Cape Vincent
Steamer "St. Lawrence".... to Alexandria Bay
Richelieu & Ontario Nav. Co .... to Kingston
Grand Trunk R'y.. to Midland and Georgian Bay

ROUTE RETURNING:

Grand Trunk R'y................... to Toronto
Grand Trunk R'y............. to Niagara Falls
West Shore R.R .... to Oneida Castle
New York, Ont. & West'n R'y.... to New York
Rate from New York................. $32 75

Exc. No. 33, Forms 385 and 386— ALEXANDRIA BAY and Return.

New York, Ont. & West'n R'y.to Central Square
Rome, Water'n & Ogd'g R.R .... to Clayton
Steamer .... to Alexandria Bay

Returning via same route.

Rates from New York.. { Single, $8 75
{ Excursion, 16 00

SUMMER EXCURSION ROUTES.

Exc. No. 34, Form 333—CAPE VINCENT and Return.

New York, Ont. & West'n R'y. to Central Square
Rome, Water'n & Ogd'g R.R.. to Cape Vincent
Returning via same route.

Rates from New York.. { Single, $8 20 / Excursion, 14 50

Exc. No. 35, Form 27—CLAYTON and Return.

New York, Ont. & West'n R'y. to Central Square
Rome, Water'n & Ogd'g R.R.. to Cape Vincent
Steamer...........................to Clayton
Returning via same route.

Rates from New York.. { Single, $8 25 / Excursion, 15 25

Exc. No. 36, Form 27—THOUSAND ISLANDS PARK and Return.

New York, Ont. & West'n R'y. to Central Square
Rome, Water'n & Ogd'g R.R.. to Cape Vincent
Steamer "St. Lawrence".. to Thousand Islands Park.
Returning via same route.

Rates from New York.. { Single, $8 60 / Excursion, 16 00

Exc. No. 37, Form 334—THOUSAND ISLANDS, MUSKOKA LAKES and Return.

(Returning via Niagara Falls.)

New York, Ont. & West'n R'y. to Central Square
Rome, Water'n & Ogd'g R.R... to Cape Vincent
Steamer "St. Lawrence"....to Alexandria Bay
Richelieu & Ontario Nav. Co ......to Kingston
Grand Trunk R'y........................to Orilla
Northern & Northwest R.R.. to Muskoka Wharf
Northern & Northwest R.R...........to Toronto
Steamer "Empress of India"..to Pt. Dalhousie
Grand Trunk R'y..............to Niagara Falls
West Shore R.R................to Oneida Castle
New York, Ont. & West'n R'y....to New York

Rates from New York...............$31 75

Exc. No. 38, Forms 309 and 310—KINGSTON, ONT. and Return.

New York, Ont. & West'n R'y. to Central Square
Rome, Water'n & Ogd'g R.R,.. to Cape Vincent
St. Lawrence Steamboat Co........to Kingston
Returning via same route.

Rates from New York.. { Single, $9 20 / Excursion, 16 00

LAKE MOHONK.

Exc. No. 39, Forms 254 and 255—LAKE MOHONK.

New York, Ont. & West'n R'y. to Campbell Hall
Wallkill Valley R.R...............to New Paltz
Smiley's Stage.................to Lake Mohonk
Returning via same route.

Rates from New York.. { Single, $3 46 / Excursion, 6 40

LAKE MINNEWASKA.

Exc. No. 40, Forms 252 and 253—LAKE MINNEWASKA.

New York, Ont. & West'n R'y to Campbell Hall
Wallkill Valley R.R...............to New Paltz
Smiley's Stage.................to Minnewaska
Returning via same route.

Rates from New York.. { Single, $3 71 / Excursion, 6 30

WATKINS GLEN.

Exc. No. 41, Form 48—WATKINS GLEN and Return.

New York, Ont. & West'n R'y.......to Oneida
N. Y. C. & H. R. R.R..............to Geneva
Seneca Lake Steamers.. ....to Watkins
Returning via same route.

Rate from New York $11 75

Exc. No. 42, Form 47—WATKINS GLEN and Return.

ROUTE GOING:
New York, Ont. & West'n R'y.......to Oneida
West Shore R.R...................to Canastota
Elmira, Cortlandt & Northern R.R...to Elmira
Northern Central R.R..............to Watkins

ROUTE RETURNING:
Seneca Lake Steamers ....to Geneva
N. Y. C. & H. R. R.R ....to Oneida
New York, Ont. & West'n R'y....to New York

Rate from New York................$12 75

Exc. No. 43—WHITE LAKE and Return.

New York, Ont. & West'n R'y ......to Liberty
Stanton's Stage.................to White Lake
Returning via same route.

Rates from New York.. { Single, / Excursion,

REDUCE your Coal Bills. . . . .
IT'S EASY if you use the Celebrated .

ONTARIO AND **COAL.** WESTERN

ASK YOUR DEALER to fill your order with this Celebrated Coal. . . . .

DICKSON & EDDY, General Sales Agents,
29 BROADWAY, NEW YORK.

NEXT FALL

When you return from your Summer Outing, tell your dealer to furnish you with

ONTARIO AND WESTERN

COAL

NONE BETTER.

DICKSON & EDDY,

General Sales Agents,

29 BROADWAY,—————— NEW YORK.